THE FIVE PILLAR METHOD

LIVING ORGANIZED TO DECLUTTER YOUR LIFE, HOME, AND MIND

LEAH NOVAK

CONTENTS

INTRODUCTION

Dear Reader:

In my life, I have had many hats to wear. I have been a student, a wife, a caretaker, a single mother, then a wife and a married mother again. I am also a daughter, a sister, an aunt, a team leader, and many, many more things. I'm the shoulder to cry on for my family, I'm the one to rely on at work, and I'm the one who has to step up to the plate to make sure everything is organized and ready to go.

But I wasn't always like that.

There were days that left my head spinning and other days when all I wanted to do was sit down and pull my hair out, those days where I couldn't take one more question, disruption, or distraction without giving up completely on whatever I was doing. We've all been there. But then I would have days when I was excelling at work, school, and mothering so fantastically that I would want to high-five everyone I saw (I didn't, but I did want to).

Everything seemed to fall into place.

But that span of time where I had things "under control" was minuscule when compared to the times when I didn't feel like I could keep my head above water and felt like everything was spinning into chaos. The bad times far outweighed the good ones, and the struggle to catch my breath was real, scary, and at times debilitating.

That is why I stopped.

I stopped in the middle of the whirling dervish of havoc, and I said, *enough*. I had to find a way to get everything situated so I didn't always feel as though I was getting ready to jump right off the rails. It was time that I made a plan to do this, for my family and for myself.

So I made a list.

I like lists. Not everyone does, but I do. I find that making lists helps me organize my thoughts and keep track of what I have to do. They get the words and the ideas out of my head to make room for new ones. So, step one of making my plan was to sit down and write a list of the most important things in my life. My list looked like this:

1. Home
2. Work
3. Finances
4. Social
5. Health

Under "home," I wanted to get my house in order, so my living environment matched how I wanted my brain to work. I spent a lot of time at home; I didn't want to spend that time worrying about how it looked or what still needed to be done inside and outside of the house. Under "work," I knew getting more organized would alleviate the mounting stress and help me take some of the tasks off my plate. When I looked at my "finances," I knew that I wanted to pay my bills on time and make sure that I saved a little for the kids so we could have fun. For "social," I wanted to make time for the kids and my friends, and make time for my husband so we didn't drift apart. And, for my "health," I wanted to make healthy food choices and start exercising, as well as see my therapist when I needed a shoulder to lean on instead of taking it all on myself.

Once I wrote my goals down, I realized that these five lists were like pillars, keeping everything standing and supporting each other in tandem. I saw the importance of developing a balance in these areas, and I developed a method so I would be able to put everything in place, all while still living my life and doing what I had to do.

More often than not, kids live the life that they are shown. While no one's life is perfect, if I could show my children that if I could make it work, then they would pick up on healthy habits and their lives could be less chaotic than mine as they grow into adults.

Putting these pillars into action first meant that I had to do some research. When the kids were with their father and when I had a moment to myself, I looked online and found that there was psychology to clutter—and not just clutter in your physical area, but also clutter in your mind, in the online environments you frequent, creeping into your finances, and saturating your personal life with white noise and distractions. Bit by bit, I found what was cluttering up my life, and like a house, brick by brick, I would build on what was solid and resolve to shore up or discard my weak links.

I set goals and deadlines for myself, charting everything out, and began to put my plan in motion. It didn't happen overnight—it took everything I had to make it happen the next day. Instead of walking by a basket of laundry in the basement, I took it upstairs, folded it, and put it away. I looked at the unpaid bills sitting on my dining room table, took the whole bundle of mail, and separated it into bills, letters, junk, and so on. I resolved to pay those bills when I had time later that evening to get them out in the next morning's mail. Small steps, but I took a look back two weeks later and saw what I'd been missing for a long time: *progress*. Moving forward, getting things together, some kind of *change*. It felt good, so I resolved to keep it up. I found other small ways to be proactive in my home life: doing dishes, cleaning and organizing cupboards, and tackling things as I saw them. I didn't stop and say "I don't have time for that." I *made* time, and that's what made it work.

One day at a time, step by step, I did one thing for each pillar, and soon, I found that those days that I was on the verge of going nuts were fewer and farther between. I had found a unique method that helped me handle things and helped balance my life.

Now I want to share this method with you.

Life has this awkward way of telling you what the problem is without ever saying a word. The work doesn't slow down when you are struggling. It is up to us to keep on top of everything life throws our way. By bringing balance to your five life pillars, you develop confidence so that when something goes sideways, you'll be able to effectively manage it and make sure it doesn't become too overwhelming. Whatever that problem is, you can give it your whole, undivided attention when you don't have other things going on, bouncing around in the back of your head and reminding you that you didn't pay those bills, you didn't do that laundry, and you didn't make time for what was important to you.

Now it's your turn. It's time for you to take steps in your life and get started to find a way to manage your life pillars. First things first, you'll need to find where your clutter is. Is it just your home needing to be organized or do you find that upon reflection your finances need work too? When was the last time you thought about your health? What you are eating, how you are sleeping at night, do you need twelve cups of coffee just to get through work? These aren't easy questions to ask yourself. But this is one of the best places to start, and this is what helped me: you map out what keeps your life standing and map out how you want to approach each piece.

I want to show you that clutter is more than inanimate objects lying around the house. Instead, clutter is anything that you can see or feel peripherally that takes your attention away from where you want your focus to be. It's not always on the surface, but it can be bubbling under; it can be mounting debt, toxic relationships, lack of quality sleep, or poor eating habits.

Follow along with me on these steps of self-discovery to find out what your clutter is and clear a path forward for a manageable life and a healthier, happier you.

> *"You will never be completely ready. Start from wherever you are."*
>
> C.J. HAYDEN

With warmest regards,

Leah Novak

PSYCHOLOGY OF CLUTTER

"Good order is the foundation of all things."

EDMUND BURKE

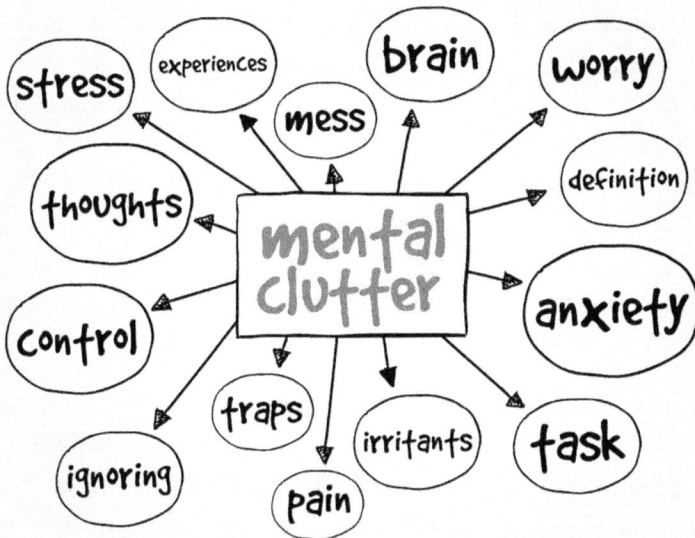

YOU COME HOME after a long day with arms full of groceries needing to be put away. You look around, but you can't put them down anywhere. *There's just too much stuff in here!* you think to yourself. Your kitchen is filled with physical clutter.

When you are lying in bed at night, unable to stop the incessant thoughts buzzing around in your head, and you are stressing out and thinking to yourself, *Why can't I just go to sleep?* your mind is filled with mental clutter.

It's no secret, clutter disrupts your life.

What most do not understand is how deep the rabbit hole actually goes. When you become overwhelmed with clutter, chances are you stop paying attention to it altogether, stop trying to figure out what went wrong, and start ignoring all the things that were once important to you because it all blends together with the everyday activities you are desperately trying to keep under control.

Clutter, whether you know it or not, comes in many forms. There's the mental clutter of a mind overwhelmed, there's the emotional clutter that comes from stress and suppressed emotions, and there's the physical clutter that piles up around you when your life is on hold. At the same time, you try to push everything down. You try to get things "organized" but instead end up giving in to "organized chaos" and figure that is how things will always be for you. Over time, day after day, you become lethargic and tired. Instead of focusing on the mess that surrounds you, you can't seem to get up when you need to, your work begins to slack, and you're apathetic to what was once important to you.

If your living space isn't clear, then your brain probably isn't either. A healthy state of mind comes from a healthy environment. This idea goes the other way as well. If you've ever switched on your phone or laptop and thought, *I don't even know what's on here anymore,* the chances are that your life needs a clean-out. The same thing goes with social media. Stop and think about it for a second: how many "friends" do you actually have on your social media accounts? Say you have 500 "friends"—do you even interact with them? Do you know them as a person? Do they post toxic content? Would you want them in your daily, physical life knocking at your door?

If not, think about how mentally exhausting that is: you're spending your time keeping up with people online who don't know you, and you don't know them either. Chances are you might not even want to! Your time and energy is better used elsewhere.

How Clutter Hurts Your Health

Clutter is overwhelmingly bad for you, but sometimes having a bit of clutter is normal. But if the clutter doesn't serve a purpose, chances are, you are not functioning to the best of your ability. If you accumulate more and more items you have no real use for, become isolated because you don't want anyone to see all the mess, or even have a pest infestation because of the clutter, you have a problem on your hands.

Think of it this way: your physical environment is a reflection of your mental environment, so with that in mind, what does that say about how you are doing?

Dr. Sherrie Bourg Carter, a doctor of psychology and an author of the effects of women and stress, discusses other ideas of how clutter can play a significant role in our health and well-being. While she says that clutter can cause stress, relieving your physical space of the clutter can be easy if you just prioritize organizing. Other types of clutter, such as mental clutter, can be cleared away by using her most basic and useful tip—focus on one project at a time without the interference of cell phones, emails, or other electronic gadgets.

Her explanation includes eight reasons why stress can be messy. Clutter promotes hyper-awareness of everything surrounding us. The excessive stimuli bombards your senses, which causes them to work overtime on items that aren't important. Clutter divides your attention, makes it harder to relax, makes you anxious, guilt-trips you, makes you feel like you're never done working, stifles your creativity, and of course makes you more prone to losing things.

Anxiety Mixed with a Cluttered Space Causes More Anxiety

As we know, it is well-documented through research that our physical environments greatly influence the way our brain works, how emotional we get, and how we behave. Researchers have conducted various tests in 2011 and 2009 showing how this influence translates over to other people we are in relationships with.

The human brain finds patterns in everything. It was an important trait for our ancestors (since a caveman who can't see the pattern of a venomous snake he's about to step on probably wouldn't have lasted very long), and we can still see how important it is in the modern day. We use this trait both in work, such as using grid line patterns to break up a table or piece of graph paper, and in play, through things like Sudoku puzzles, crosswords, and finding clouds with odd shapes in the sky. No matter what you tell yourself, your brain needs an order of some kind, a way to pick out information, patterns, and visual cues from your environment. It's logical, then, that order with material objects is a constant visual reminder of how well we are doing in life (not necessarily financially, but in congruence with other aspects—an expensive cabinet covered in papers, wires, and other small items isn't any better for being expensive, instead it just becomes a messy, expensive junk holder). When things are out of order in your house, at work, in your car, and so on, your brain is unable to focus on one item. The visual distraction will drain cognitive resources and reduce your ability to have a fully functioning brain and use your working memory as you need it.

Cognitive overload happens when your home and work life is overloaded to the point where your stress levels shoot upward. At the same time, your capacity to take in information and absorb it cognitively is severely lessened. There is also the effect of a continuous fight or flight response when living in a chronically cluttered environment. This trigger can affect physical and psychological issues that have an impact on how your body fights illnesses, digests food, and can pump up your risk for heart disease and type 2 diabetes.

Clutter can even affect the way you read emotions. A study conducted in 2016 found that participants were unable to interpret emotional expressions of characters in rooms that had a background of clutter. Their brains were more distracted by extra items around the room and couldn't focus properly on the faces of the people they were supposed to be looking at. Likewise, it's been discovered that when there is too much clutter, you might not realize that your visual cortex is overwhelmed at the sight of your items out of place. When you begin to feel overwhelmed, it can paralyze you into a state of doing nothing.

These findings increase the idea that clutter and messiness are linked with negative emotions and irritability; an organized home can eliminate some of these symptoms.

This cognitive dysfunction doesn't stop when you are ready for sleep. If your bedroom is cluttered, you probably have problems sleeping. You may not be able to fall asleep, or you may not be able to stay asleep. Many studies have linked disorganized lives and messy environments to poor eating habits. Why find a healthy snack in the mess of a kitchen where cookies and chips are readily sitting out? Plus the rush of instant gratification can seem like a reward when really it's your brain behaving badly with the poor habits you've built over the years.

When your kitchen is dirty or disorganized, the chances of you reaching for cookies instead of healthier snacks rises, along with the fact that you may be eating twice as many of those unhealthier snacks.

Other studies show a 77 percent chance of someone being over-weight in an exceedingly cluttered home. People who have hoarding tendencies can actually have a physical reaction to throwing things away. This reaction comes from the brain and is associated with physical pain.

On the other side of the spectrum, it may seem crazy, but there are people who clean to make themselves feel better. Keeping a home and work environment clean can lighten your mood, relieve frustration, and give an overall sense of calmness. Evidence found in a 2009 study in the *Personality and Social Psychology Bulletin* discovered women who lived in clean homes were found to be more restful and restored. On the other hand, women with unfinished projects and built-up clutter were said to be more depressed and fatigued.

When a person is depressed, the symptoms can include a hopeless outlook, a loss of interest in hobbies, issues with sleep and fatigue, anxiety, physical pain, weight gain, distraction, confusion, apathy, and constant tension. After everything we've covered, this might sound familiar. You might be thinking of someone you know, maybe even yourself.

The Benefits of Cleaning Your Clutter

There is evidence that clearing your clutter positively affects your mental health as well. One of the main reasons is that having a clean private space can give you a sense of control over the place you live in, and it can engage your mind in repetitive activities, which can have a positive and calming effect. Cleanliness can also improve your mood with a sense of accomplishment and satisfaction.

Benefits Physical Health

Indiana University published a study written by Dr. NiCole Keith, who found that people in better shape had more organized homes. Keith found that cleanliness is a better predictor of a healthy person than how often they get outside to go for a walk around the neighborhood.

How does knowing that being proactive in your environment can keep you healthy and fit without having to suit up for a morning jog? Feels good, right?

Environmental Control

We lack control over many things in life, which can bring on its own form of anxiety. Some people bake when they're stressed, or they might have a nap, listen to music, or give attention to pets or plants. Some people clean when they're stressed, and it's because cleaning can help people get a sense of mastery over their environment. When you keep your environment clean, you can take back control in one area of your life even if the rest of it looks pretty bleak.

The University of Connecticut found that in times of high stress, many often default to behaviors where there is a repetitive motion, such as cleaning, because it allows them to focus on a specific task rather than the chaos surrounding them.

The opposite is said with spaces that are clutter-filled and disorganized. These areas will make focusing harder, so you avoid projects and it leaves you feeling like you're in a rut. Have you found you are avoiding financial, health, or social responsibilities due to being mentally drained or overwhelmed?

Mood Improvement

By removing disorganization, you can start reducing your anxiety right away, providing you with a positive mood boost.

A journal article published in *Mindfulness* that found people took things more slowly when washing the dishes. They took time to make dishwashing an experience, like smelling the soap or really paying attention to the feel and temperature of the water. Learning to take pleasure in the little things is what life is all about. Even with the most mundane tasks we can still find enjoyment, and sometimes that's a really easy thing to forget. This study discovered that when participants were washing the dishes, there was a 27 percent reduction in their anxiety, and an increase in feeling inspired mentally for 25 percent of the group.

Even clean sheets are associated with a better night's sleep, which improves your mood all on its own. Changing your bedsheets out once every two weeks can reduce fatigue, anxiety, stress, and depression.

Increase Your Focus

It makes sense that chaos detracts from your focus. It also limits your brain's ability to process information. Research has found that the more organized your home is, the more productive you actually are. Another way to look at it is, if you are having issues focusing, declutter the area you are trying to finish your project in. Devoting just a few minutes to clear a space can help you be more productive and direct your focus better by limiting any personal items that vie for your attention instead.

Ask yourself what's bothering you. Does it have an easy fix? Resolving these small things will give you the encouragement to tackle the larger issues. It may sound like a no-brainer to put your keys on a key hook, but it might surprise you how hard building that habit can be when you haven't worked at it or when you've only just picked it up. If you find keys drifting from table to table, cabinet to cabinet, only to disappear one day and reappear the next like a magician's trick, remember that reinforcing that habit is key (quite literally) to make sure that it sticks and the keys stay on that key hook where they're supposed to be!

So after all that, where do you start cleaning up the mess that surrounds you?

Declutter your life.

2

THE FIVE PILLAR METHOD

*"There is a beautiful world of freedom and fresh breath
   hiding behind that clutter.
Deciding how to declutter your home is up to you."*

JOSHUA BECKER

WHEN YOU DECIDE to clean up your life, you might just think that means moving some of the piles of dirty plates into the dishwasher, putting books back on the shelf and off that chair you've been piling them on, or finding that missing left sock that disappeared in the laundry last Tuesday. We need to look beyond that.

Just reshuffling the items in your house isn't going to help you find clarity and things won't fall magically into place because you finally recovered that missing sock. What *will* help is taking a step-by-step approach to each portion of your life. I've broken these up into five "pillars": home, work, money, social, and health. These are five broad categories that just about everyone can relate to. Most people go wrong by stopping at the home: they don't understand that there's so much more that affects your life than toys lying on your living room floor, overstuffed closets, or messy coffee tables.

Within these five pillars are important parts of each subject. Within your money pillar, for example, we have budgeting, which is crucial for a lot of people to make ends meet. This important part of the money pillar merits a five-step method: assess where you are currently, evaluate what you want to change, plan to make that change, take action to implement your plan, and reassess where you are at the end. Five pillars supporting your life, five steps for working in each pillar. With the Five Pillar Method, assessing and reassessing is always an important part because you need to see where you are and where you want to be.

Assess Your Clutter

You now have an understanding of the positive benefits of clearing your clutter away and it can give you a new outlook on life. Now it's time to assess your clutter. Remember, clutter isn't just tripping over trash or stepping on a Lego block on the way to the bathroom; it's also the stuff that you think about, the social media notifications collected on your phone, and the unreturned texts asking you to do something.

The Five Pillar Method breaks down the five main parts of your life to help you become more organized. But first, we have to start small. This practice isn't something you will be able to snap your fingers at and everything will magically disappear. Instead, it takes exactly what it sounds like: *practice*. You can think of it as a board game where you have to take on tasks, complete missions, and then get to the next block. Each block will be a new task and mission, and then once you get all the way to the end of the board, you'll know how to use the Five Pillar Method to best suit your own life.

This block is to help you assess where your clutter is coming from and will have you asking yourself if you have a *simple* fix for some of your messiest problems. It doesn't have to be complicated: if you have papers everywhere, is it because they have nowhere else to go? Can you start with putting them in a filing cabinet or do you need to get one? If you have problems keeping your spices in one place, can you get a spice rack? If you have problems keeping your keys in one place, install a key hook by the front door and start leaving keys there every day.

Life is about balance, and it's more complex than you might think.

As an example, your work life is not just sitting at your desk. You'd be surprised to know that it also includes your coworker relationships and taking a much-needed lunch break for yourself. As you start picking apart each pillar and categorizing accordingly, you will see things falling into place, and you will find that you have more time for doing the things that you love to do the most—including hobbies, "you" time, and that one thing you say you always "should" do, but never have the time to.

Overstimulation is easy. Unwinding and untying yourself from being overstimulated from any of these aspects in life takes a bit of dedication and the right mindset, but it can be done!

Think Like A Minimalist, but Be True to Your Lifestyle

The Five Pillar Method doesn't have to do with changing up your lifestyle so much that you become a different person. Instead, it's about thinking of terms in checks and balances. When I say to think like a minimalist, I don't mean start throwing everything in the garbage if it doesn't bring you any joy or happiness in your life. Take this opportunity to think about the clutter in your five life pillars, and realize that there are many things you can improve to streamline your day and free up time.

Minimalism, by definition, is letting go of things that don't serve you, optimizing your life to how you want it, and freeing up more time to enjoy what life has to offer. When you are a minimalist, you don't keep things just because someone gave them to you. You can't keep items just because you might use them one day.

Living a simple life with less possessions sounds amazing, especially when you are eliminating excess baggage you no longer use or need. Decluttering is key. Think about it this way:

1. You'll have less to clean and organize.
2. You'll have less stress.
3. You'll have more financial freedom and less debt.
4. You'll find more energy to pursue your dreams.

Sounds good, right?

Once you get the hang of cleaning and decluttering, remember you don't have to go overboard with it. The Five Pillar Method is about finding balance, which you can't do if you spend all your time cleaning up after yourself or everyone else. (And again, I'm not just talking about being at home: working hard is good, spending is inevitable, and you're going to eat junk food at some point—and that's okay, so long as it's all in a good, healthy balance!) Plus, life events are rarely planned, and some things just don't go according to plan—that's okay too, because life is all about expecting the unexpected.

Your Five Steps to Success

As discussed previously, each pillar has five steps, where you will assess what is wrong, evaluate what you want, plan how to achieve your goals, take action, and assess your progress. We'll go through these steps in detail for each pillar, but rather than jumping into it all at once, let's look at an outline of what you'll see in each chapter.

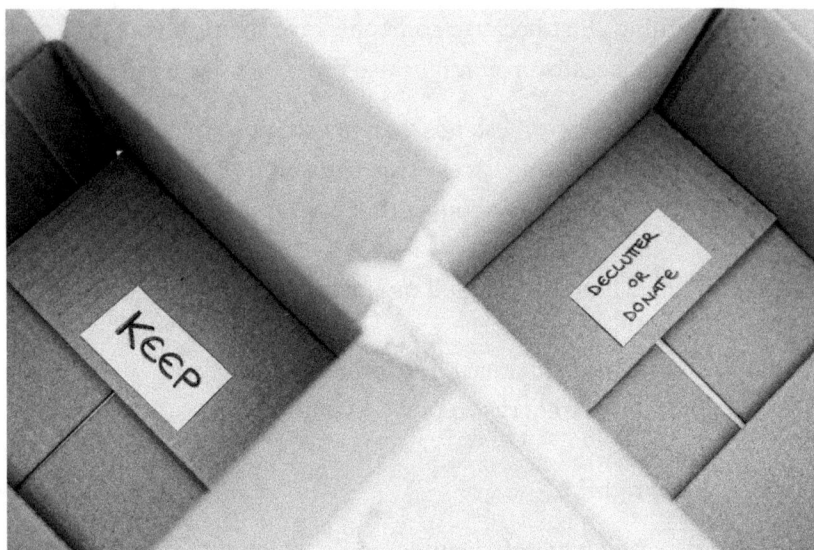

Assess Your Situation

Take the time to sit down and assess where you are right now. What is wrong in your home, work, or social pillar? Where can you improve in each area of your life? Do you think the problem is your lack of time? Could the issue be that you are not communicating your goals with your family, friends, or the people who can help? Do you think you have a problem implementing the rules after you set them? Are you easily distracted?

Evaluate What You Want

So you know where you're at right now. Now think about where you *want* to be. What kind of progress do you want to see? Think about what you want and write it down. When you write down your ideas, you can see what your thoughts are. When you see something, it is easier to make it become a reality. If you are a visual person, consider creating a vision board that includes pictures of how you'd like your home to look.

Plan How to Organize (and Get Results)

Now you know what you want, but you need a plan of action to get it! Perhaps you created your vision board with images and articles of how you'd like to keep your home, or wrote down goals for your health. Now, how are you going to get the results you want?

When you plan out your actions, even if they don't always go accordingly, you can find the steps you need to take to put your plan in motion. This step is half the battle. The second half will be to hold yourself accountable for the actions you take.

Utilize one digital or physical calendar where you will store all your tasks with the date and time to complete them. For example, if you plan to clean your kitchen this week, break up the task into small sections for each day of the week:

- Monday: Organize utensils.
- Tuesday: Sort pots and pans.
- Wednesday: Clean out pantry.
- Thursday: Sort out under the sink.
- Friday: Deep clean the kitchen.

Set a timer and dedicate forty-five minutes to the task each day. Acquire a minimum of three boxes: Toss, Keep, and Donate for your target area.

Take Action

When you take action, you will be starting on the process of clearing away your clutter—in all forms—and while doing so, you'll also be building up your routine to keep things orderly. Remember, set a timer for forty-five minutes before you begin your chosen task. Doing this trains your brain to adopt a certain mindset and a routine, and you will be more successful in completing your tasks over time.

As you come to clean and sort out each pillar, you will throw things away, delete things, or close out accounts; and put items in boxes, folders, or files—in essence, you'll put them in organized "closed" spaces. When you are done with your organization and removing clutter for the day, take a step back and note how differently the area looks, how it feels, and see how hard the task was to start, but easy once you got going.

You're going to be feeling better. You will be able to take deeper breaths and feel more relaxed in your space. You will achieve that sense of accomplishment you crave. Remember this is where *you* hold yourself accountable for implementing steps. If you do not continue to press on and build on the momentum of your organization, then you will not succeed.

That being said, taking action doesn't mean that you won't miss a day or get busy with an important life event. But you have to be *honest* with yourself, and for some, that's not always easy.

Finish up taking action by being honest with yourself about how hard organizing or cleaning the section was. The difficulty of doing an action should not include whether you *felt* like doing it or not. It's better to focus on the level of difficulty it took to do the action—including how long it took, how much heavy lifting you did, and your stress level while you were organizing.

A good way to track this will be to keep a personalized, interactive journal about what you accomplished and how you felt while you were cleaning. By keeping a written record of your work and your progress, you'll be able to see your success unfold. If you are a visual person, a photographic record can be helpful. Consider taking before and after pictures on your phone or camera.

Once you get into the habit of organizing (keep in mind that it takes an average of twenty-one days to form a habit), you will start to get a yearning to do it, even if you miss the occasional day here and there.

Reassess Your Progress

For this step, not only do you have to be honest with yourself, but you also have to come up with solutions to fix issues.

Now, honesty doesn't mean that you beat yourself up for a job that you didn't do. Honesty means that you will say, *Yes, I took shortcuts to get this done,* or *Yes, I didn't do the best I could,* or *Yes, I skipped some steps,* and then you give yourself ways to make it better next time.

When you reassess your progress at the end of each week, consider the following questions:

1. How are you doing so far? Have you gotten partway, halfway, or all the way done with what you set out to do?
2. How are you feeling? Did you do a good job, or do you think you could improve?
3. What is the biggest project you've tackled? How did you do it? Is it a method that you can use when you're working on your next project?
4. What will your next goal be?

Be firm but forgiving with yourself. Holding yourself accountable in your reassessment means that you *will* make it better next time. Don't take this as a chance for you to debase yourself on a daily basis because you *didn't* do something. Instead, it's an opportunity to do things *better*.

3

HOME IS WHERE THE HEART IS

"Have nothing in your house that you do not know to be useful or believe to be beautiful."

WILLIAM MORRIS

LET'S back up for a minute and meet Jacqueline. Her story may sound familiar to some.

Jacqueline is a married mother of three. Her life is busy, to say the least. Between juggling homework, dance lessons, meals, and running a household, she sometimes feels she is drowning in obligations.

Her job first and foremost is being a mom, but she wishes she could spend a little less time on the work she does and a little more on enjoying what she has now: her family, her friends, and her health. The never-ending to-do list has stopped her from seeing friends, eating well, even having date nights with her husband. She knows if she could just take back control, everything else would fall into place, but she doesn't know where to start. Her life has been organized chaos for so long she doesn't know any other way to live. She doesn't have time for herself, let alone anything extra.

She knows that when you're a mom, your job is never done, but her stress levels are so high she finds herself lying awake at night, leaving her overly tired and stressed for the following day. Sometimes she snaps at the kids or her husband, and she feels guilty but isn't quite sure how to control herself again. She wants to know where the balance is so she can make the most out of her family life.

Home life has to do with the physical space of the home, your possessions, your family, and the basic needs of a fulfilling life. You should have the time for volunteering and religious events, time spent taking care of the family, and downtime for yourself as well. But not everything goes as planned. Statistics show that one in four Americans will describe themselves as "super stressed," which is a far cry from being healthy, happy, or balanced.

Chronic Stress and the Home

Stress can be helpful sometimes: it encourages you to push yourself and do your best, and you might find that you do better with that extra push to impress your boss or your friends with your hard work. However, when that stress is constant, day in and day out, it stops being beneficial and starts draining you.

When you stress out, your productivity will drop and you may become irritable, depressed, or even self-sabotaging. Eventually, your immune system will begin to fail too, which will bring on all sorts of ailments, from colds to heart disease. It is documented that chronic stress will double your risk of a heart attack.

So, how do you get that balance back? See a few of the tips below:

- **Delegate, delegate, delegate**. Even young children can have little chores they can help with. Ensure that the home responsibilities are evenly distributed and that it adheres to age-appropriate tasks. Have the tasks clearly outlined by writing the responsibilities on a dry-erase board, having a daily conversation, or developing a good way to communicate with your family.
- **Reach out to others**. Chances are there are others in your social circle that have similar issues. Reach out to your family and friends and talk about your issues. Listen to their advice and implement it in the best way that will work for you.
- **Unplug from electronics**. Give yourself time away from technology. If you work in an office, you probably spend a lot of time looking at a computer screen. Then you come home to a TV, a tablet, or a phone. A constant need for interaction with technology will burn you out quickly.
- **Stop overscheduling**. Your kids don't have to have an activity every day. You don't have to jam your schedule full of events, work, and chores just to feel productive. Putting extra tasks on your calendar because you can't say no when other people request your time puts extra stress on you! Telling yourself that you "have to stay busy" might mean

that you are avoiding something. Neither is a healthy approach to your time or your life.

Look around your house and assess where you have clutter. If you look at something and say, "Hmm, I don't think there's an easy fix for this one," then make a note of it and come back to it later. Your goal right now is simple, easy fixes. Consider these tips when going through your home:

- **Go digital:** Too many receipts clutter up a space for basically no reason. Consider going digital with receipts to keep track of your finances. Most financial institutions and businesses have an online presence now. Ask to receive email or text receipts, and utilize your bank account's online features. The paperwork around the house will lessen (plus, it's a bonus for the environment).
- **Color-code everything:** Getting colored items for each person (especially kids) in the house will add an extra fun step to the process and is a simple way to know whose belongings are whose. Does your child have a favorite color? They can take responsibility for their purple toothbrush and purple blanket and purple boots! You can do this with toothbrushes, hairbrushes, clothing items and toys, kids' plates and utensils, cubbies, and more.
- **Hangers, anyone?** Do you like fashion and have accessories to match each outfit? Create an outfit all on one space-saving hanger or combination pants and shirt hanger fit with loops and spacers. When you add accessories to one hanger to complete an outfit, it will eliminate the time you spend searching for something to wear, and you will also get a chance to condense your cluttered closet.
- **Folding linens:** When you wash your bedsheets and pillowcases, fold all items except one pillowcase, then store the folded linens in the unfolded pillowcase. Now, you'll

have only to open a cupboard drawer and pull out one thing instead of searching around for four or five.

- **No more password Post-it:** Instead of writing passwords on Post-its and leaving them everywhere, get a small, handheld notebook that you can keep in a drawer, nightstand, or somewhere safe. Then, when you need a password, you aren't digging around through countless notes, and everything is kept in one place.

The "Home" Steps

Now we can go through the five steps to assess, evaluate, plan, take action, and reassess your home space. Remember to utilize your journal, list, or vision board, and a calendar to track your tasks.

If you're new to decluttering or you've just started trying to tackle a mountain of stuff you've been eyeing up for a while, things won't come naturally to you. Just remember, approach decluttering the same way you'd walk down a street: with one step at a time.

Assess Your Home Space

Look around your home. What do you see? What is disorganized in your environment? Do you see places where you can improve your kitchen, dining room, living room, bedrooms, and bathrooms?

If you have children, how do their rooms look? Do they have trouble with cleaning up after themselves? Do you make sure that you, as a parent, reinforce the importance of cleanliness in their rooms? Remember that organizing is a habit-building experience, so the more they do it, the easier it will be for them to learn the habit.

Does your partner respect the outcome you are trying to accomplish? How can they help? Do you have a roommate who can join in on the organization?

Ask yourself how you contribute to the clutter and mess. Where do you fit into the picture? Do you have problems implementing cleanliness? Do you become easily distracted? Are you the culprit leaving mail on the dining room table or laundry baskets around the house?

Evaluate What You Want

Now that you have an idea of how to improve your environment, it's time to evaluate what you want things to look like around your home. Ask yourself these questions:

1. How do you feel about yourself right now? What can you improve?
2. How do you see your home right now? What would you like to see?

   a) What do you want for your home?

   b) How do you want to keep a clutter-free space?

   c) What type of practices can you implement? (A couple of examples are cleaning one room or section each day, or cleaning everything on your days off.)

Write down what you want in your pillar journal, or use a vision board with pictures that can serve as inspiration. Evaluating what you want for your space will give you an attainable goal to reach for. Once you have visualized it, then you can turn it into reality with planning.

If you don't love or use it it is clutter

Plan How to Organize

If you write what you want in your journal or create your vision board, it will be easier to plan to keep your home clutter-free. Use your digital or physical calendar to keep you on track.

For the home pillar, it's best if you start small. When you assess your environment, map out what parts of your living area need to be cleaned or fixed up. Make a list of every area that you want to see clean.

Planning for Target Days

Set a deadline of getting your home cleared, cleaned, and clutter-free for twenty days.

1. The first seven days (days 1–7): Focus on *cleaning your living room*. This is likely the first thing that people see when they walk into your home, so this is logically the best place to start!

- Pick up all trinkets, trash, toys, and clutter. Make sure there are no loose items on the floor before you start.
- Clear everything off your tables, shelves, and stands. I recommend using the three-box method (one box to keep, one box to donate, and one box to go in the trash) when looking through your trinkets and clutter. Decide what can be tossed or donated, and then figure out how you want to organize what you want to keep. Ask yourself what you want to do with what's left over. Does it need to go into a storage space? Do you want it set out for use or decoration?
- Collect all "bedding" (blankets, throws, and pillows) and store extras in decorative storage bins that you've bought or repurposed.
- Got any skeletons in your closets? Then it's time to clear them out! Straighten up any closets in your living room space. Keep your closet floors tidy with a shoe rack, hang up all coats, sort accessories into a bin or cubby, and remember the back of the closet door can be turned into storage as well.

- Go through your electronic items (old phone chargers, old radios, broken cables, and dead batteries, just to name a few) and sort the ones that you want to toss or donate, then organize what you want to keep. When you're done, tie up and label loose wires.

- Organize everything you need to keep into decorative bins and baskets where possible. Using the sides of the couch, the inside of a TV stand, and other small places can make a big impact on the overall look of your living room.

- Once you've cleared your living room clutter, move out all the big furniture that you can (your tables, your bins and baskets, even the couch!), then give everything a good clean before you put it all back. You'll want to do this before you move on; having to backtrack around your whole house to do housekeeping and cleaning will make you feel daunted by the task.

2. The next seven days (days 8–14): *Clean your dining room and kitchen.* We'll do two rooms this time, starting in the dining room first.

- Take everything off of the dining room table. The table is for eating only and should only have plates, utensils, and glassware on it when people are either eating or setting the table in preparation for a meal. No other items should be on your table—don't use it for storing piles and piles of mail, papers, or other items.

- If you have a centerpiece you would like to add to the table, you can (and should) keep it there. Keep your table clear of everything except this single centerpiece. After the meal is over, make sure to clear away everything from the table.

- For any cabinets or shelves you have, keep them organized. Items on a shelf should be spaced out, and cabinets should have items stacked neatly (one thing inside the other, or on top of one another without toppling). Knicknacks, trinkets, or decorations should have space between them on shelves. Other cutlery and dishes should be organized and stacked appropriately.

For your kitchen, do the following:

- Your drawers need to be cleaned and organized. Take everything out of each drawer, throw anything in it that you don't need. Donate anything that you can, and sort through everything else. Ask yourself, *Do I use this in my kitchen? Do I need it? Do I still want it?* and use that as the basis for what goes back into the drawer and what goes into storage, gets donated, or gets thrown away. Add drawer dividers and other organizational items to stop your silverware and other items from encroaching on each other.
- Your upper cabinets should only be for items that you really don't use all that much. Keep everything that you *do* use at eye level. Make sure to clean and wipe down items *before* you put them away in your cabinets. For one, the last thing you'll want to do is attract pests to your kitchen; for another, ask yourself when was the last time that you emptied the toast crumbs out of your toaster or wiped down your electric can opener. If you can't remember, or if your item has food all over it or inside it, then it's time to do it!
- Next, clear everything off of your counters and wipe them down. Use a bowl or rack for your fruit and keep your counters as clear of other items as possible. You can also utilize the backs of cabinet doors to turn them into unexpectedly spacious shelves! You can hang spice racks, paper towel holders, and small baggie boxes in little spaces like these.
- Take out any mats, pet bowls, or other items that are on the kitchen floor (make sure you clean these as needed too),

then sweep and mop the floor when you're finished as a final touch.

3. The next five days (days 15–20): *Clean your bathrooms and bedroom.* Again, two or more rooms this time and a bit less time to work on them than we've given previously. Don't feel stressed! Take a look at the following for your bathrooms:

- Clean your bathroom and store any cleaning supplies in a sturdy bin under your bathroom sink. Use a bin with a handle to make it easier to pull out all the supplies you'll need at once. Make sure that space under the sink is organized into sections and that everything has a place.
- Are you the person who has no proper place for towels? Time to break the habit! Install and use towel racks or shelves on the back of the bathroom door or wall.
- Keep your closets organized. Use baskets or bins to hold medicines and safety supplies, hair and beauty products, and other toiletries.
- Color-code or label your toiletries. Using separate baskets for each person, color-code them by making them each person's favorite color or by putting their name on it.
- Consider the unused spaces on the back of the cabinet doors, in the shower, and on the walls for more storage.
- Remember to do a deep clean of the bathroom before moving on!

For your bedroom, do the following:

- Pick up everything off the floor, down to the last pair of shoes or stray sock, and put it out of sight and in a tidy place.
- Your bedroom will need to have the closet and dressers cleaned out and organized. Go through your clothes and

your closets. Donate anything you haven't worn for six months or more. If something has a hole or is ruined, throw it away. Otherwise, make sure that your clothes, hangers, and shoes are organized.

- Sort through your accessories. You may have a lot or you may only have a few. Go through them now and pick out the ones that are your favorites, the ones you wanted for a special occasion that has long since passed, and the ones you didn't even know were there. If it's ruined, throw it away. If you don't like it, donate it. If you use it frequently or if you *really* need to keep it (ask yourself honestly why you're keeping it), set it aside to be stored in a bin, basket, or on a hanger.
- Refresh your bedding and put down clean sheets. Store bedding in one place, such as in a drawer or basket out of sight.
- If you have a nightstand, keep it minimal. Go through and organize the drawers. If you've been stuffing random items in there and haven't looked at them for a long time, it's time to clear them out. Have only your bedside lamp on top of the nightstand and aim to keep other bedtime necessities like a journal, book, or medications in the drawers.
- At the end of the tidying up process, clean and dust the room, let some light in, and open the windows for some fresh air.

On the twenty-first day, you will go back to reassess what you've cleaned, how you've kept it clear, and what you can do better.

There is a possibility that you're not in a space that's entirely yours to clean and redesign. If that is the case, then you may have to come up with ground rules for the shared spaces of your environment like the living room or dining room. Talk to that person openly and honestly, and you can both come up with a happy medium. There is no reason to get upset with them for not wanting to get on board, but don't feel the need to cater to or clean up after them either.

Take Action

Since you created your plan, you can now put it into action. Using a calendar, add a task to each day on your calendar following your plan of action. Adding the areas that need to be cleaned to each day of your calendar will help you visualize how long it will take and allow you to cross the completed item off on your calendar. Add how long you think it should take you to complete the task compared to how long it actually takes. This practice helps give you a more realistic understanding of how long it will take to reach your goal.

Follow your plan accordingly. Keep in mind doing anything over forty-five minutes on days that you work will be challenging. Focusing on cleaning up your space will take a lot of energy, and remember to pace yourself if you have pulled an eight- or twelve-hour shift.

At the end of each day, check off your journal and calendar for what you accomplished and what you will be doing the next day in preparation to keep focused on the goal ahead. Reflecting on your success with journaling or taking before and after pictures is a big motivation boost. Then reward yourself by doing something fun and relaxing. Giving yourself a break from cleaning will also implement other pillars in your life that may need attention.

Once you successfully complete your target areas, you will have to work on keeping that pace up regularly so each space doesn't get out of control. Focus on reinforcing habits like picking up any day-to-day clutter that accumulates at the end of the day. Work in a weekly cleaning routine with tasks like dusting, dishwashing, sweeping, mopping, and laundry as you go. Some of these tasks can be done once a week, such as a designated laundry day, while others, like washing the dishes, are done daily.

Reassess Your Progress

Assess your progress at the end of each week. How does your room look? Is your plan working? Where can you improve? Where did you fall short on taking action this week? What precautions can you put to avoid pitfalls you may have fallen into for the next week?

One thing to note is that you should take a step back and appreciate your progress as part of your assessment. You may find that you now have some empty space; don't try and fill it up right now, just appreciate that empty space when you're done with your work for the day. You may come back to that same space the next day and feel like it needs to have something to liven it up. *Don't* give in to that because before you know it, you've bought something you don't need and filled that space up with clutter again and upended all your hard work. Save decorating for when you've moved farther along with your decluttering, or else the decor will just become more clutter that you won't want to deal with.

The home pillar is your inner sanctuary, which will reflect how you feel about yourself. By decluttering this space, your stress will drop significantly with less clutter lying around. You'll find you have an agreeable environment to come back to, rather than a space you have to worry about returning to when you leave for work every day.

4

DON'T MAKE YOUR OWN OVERTIME

"Three Rules of Work: Out of clutter find simplicity;
From discord find harmony; In the middle of
difficulty lies opportunity."

ALBERT EINSTEIN

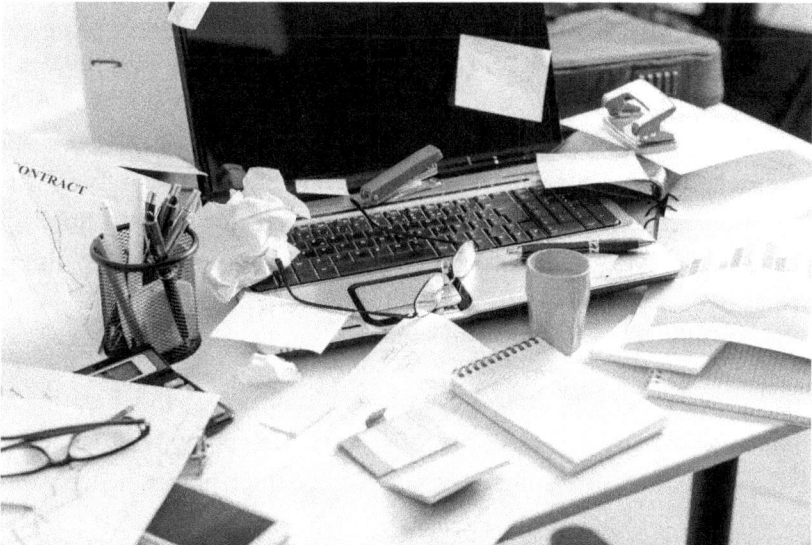

MINDY IS a twenty-eight-year-old woman who has taken the big leap in securing an apartment with her partner. She has just had some of the hardest years of her life between being laid off work and securing a direction for their future. She is ready to start over. She has been back in the workforce for only a few months and is finding it hard to balance spending time with her romantic partner, working, and keeping up with her friends. Her partner gets annoyed because she doesn't clean up around the apartment, and then there's that talk about money again. These talks often put a strain on their relationship. Mindy doesn't understand why her partner can't see that she is trying her best to keep her head above water. She wants to show her that she's trying. She's struggling and doesn't know what to do.

Work/life balance is much more than just going to work, working, and then coming home. As much as you may want it to be that easy, chances are your job is challenging, stressful, and sometimes even chaotic. When you are working outside of home, you have coworkers to contend with, your job tasks, overtime, sick days, vacation days, and the organization of your physical workspace.

There have been many definitions of what work/life balance is. In the present, being happy with your life includes having a satisfying career. When you are satisfied and challenged in your work, you have better work-life quality. The fact that you love your job should no longer mean that you ignore other parts of your life. There are many elements to balance between your life outside of work and still feeling like your work has value. Some of those have to do with the environment you work in, and others have to do with how you tackle your work, what you do with it, and how you keep things balanced for yourself.

Throughout the last fifty years, definitions have changed a little bit. In the '70s, the definition for work-life quality was the "relation of man and his task." During the '80s, work-life quality was defined as "the level to which employees can satisfy their personal needs not only in material matters but also of self-respect, contentment, and an opportunity to use their talents for personal growth."

In the '90s, the spectrum of work-life quality widened to have preferences from the individual's perspective, which included career stages, age, and position in the industry.

Today, an article titled "Quality of Work Life and Organizational Performance" was published by the *International Journal of Environmental Research and Public* stating that the QWL is connected to job satisfaction, motivation, health, safety, job security, productivity, and well-being. There are four QWL components: a safe work environment, occupational healthcare, time off work, and salary. An enormous part of QWL includes work/life balance.

Although intertwined, work/life balance and quality of work-life are not the same thing. The definition of work/life balance has evolved over the last twenty years, starting with Krichmeyer in 2000, who stated that having a work/life balance includes "achieving satisfying experiences in all life domains and [doing] so requires personal resources such as energy, time, and commitment to be well distributed across domains." By 2014, others streamlined the definition to "an individual's assessment of how well multiple life roles are balanced."

The five pillars discuss how each element of life is needed to maintain a balanced idea. Your roles—home, work, money, social, and health—all need the same, or similar, amounts of time allotted to each. Therefore, if you are a workaholic, you will cease spending enough time with your family and friends. This imbalance will ultimately lead to a less successful work/life balance.

Mindy is coming off of another hard year and started a new job about three months ago. She still feels like the "new girl" and is beginning to get nervous every time she is called to the office to talk to her supervisor. Although the supervisor never tells her anything bad about her performance, she is still shaken from her last job, which was a very toxic environment and laid her off with no warning. She is still stressed out and walks around waiting for everyone to call her out for messing something up. Because of this anxiety, she asks for extra work and never says no because she wants to prove that she is a hard-working employee who is essential to the team. She stays at work late into the night trying to complete her work and finds herself bringing it home with her, determined never to be deemed "unessential" again.

But her work life is starting to affect her home life, and her partner tries to understand, but she is also having a hard time connecting with Mindy. She is beginning to think that maybe they should see a counselor in hopes that Mindy can find some confidence again.

Obviously, Mindy is avoiding her feelings and burying herself at work, and will soon feel burned out from overloading responsibilities on herself. When that happens, she'll lose productivity, she'll stop sleeping, and then even her work will begin to suffer. She has to change something now, or she will wind up in the same place she was three months ago.

A Harvard University Professor, Richard Walton, discusses components that will impact the work-life balance. The attitude of the employee will greatly affect the outcome of how they use their time. If the employee has the right skills, knowledge, and expertise for their role, they should finish the work promptly. If they have a good attitude while doing it, they will be willing to learn more about how they can better fit into their role.

However, if they feel that their job is not secure, chances are they will feel more stressed, like Mindy.

More Is Not Always Better

Picture this: You decide to take on a new project at work. Your first step is to map out how you will achieve the finished goal. You make a list or utilize a note system, but the next day you find out your list got lost under a stack of papers somewhere, so you make another list, and then another day later when new ideas pop up. Without realizing it, you've made three lists and don't know where they are or what is on them.

So as a rule of thumb, from here on out, you will need to put calendars, planners, notes, appointments, and anything that you need to track for work in one place.

In the home pillar, you are organizing your life through a calendar and journal or vision board, and we will continue that process in the work pillar. Keep in mind, there are a lot of digital apps for tasks, checking things off, brainstorming ideas, and repetitive to-do lists, which can help you be more effective in the workplace. Consider utilizing an app that can keep up with your busy schedule both on your computer and phone.

However, if you don't like technology and have a penchant for writing things down, get one notebook with a calendar, and keep it on your desk, in your purse, or in your work bag. Check these items daily and make sure that you know what is planned for you each day.

If you find yourself feeling overwhelmed at work and aren't entirely sure why, use the list below and see if you are doing the following:

- **Focus on self-management.** Self-care includes eating, exercising, sleeping, and managing your mental health. Managing your personal care is a big part of how well you do at work. When you don't sleep well it affects your productivity, so mapping out enough time to get some shut-eye should be high up on your list. You need time for a lunch break, too—being hungry will make you less productive as well. Get out of the habit of making a fast-food restaurant your first stop for lunch. Bring a nutritious lunch with you and some healthy snacks for throughout the day.

- **Use time management.** Set goals and prioritize work tasks into different sections: what needs to be prioritized, what can be done tomorrow, and what can be done at the end of the week. Giving yourself a timeline can help you sort through the mental clutter and organize your thoughts.

- **Incorporate stress management.** Learn to adapt to an environment where distractions, conversations, and interruptions play a significant role in managing stress. Come up with three ways to adapt to the noise and distractions. For example, use a radio or playlist of relaxing music for background noise to help you improve your focus. Multitasking is highly prized as a work trait, but a lot of people do their best work when they look at one project at a time. If you can avoid multitasking projects, you'll also be able to relieve stress levels and focus on doing an excellent job on one thing at a time.

- **Manage changes.** Your company is always going to change. New people have different ideas of how things should be run, companies try to incorporate streamlined techniques, computers get upgraded, and systems change. Change is how the world works; learning to go with the flow instead of working against it will help you feel less overwhelmed. Look at the change as a learning experience, write down a list of goals you'd like to accomplish with new changes, or talk about it with a supervisor or coworker. (Instead of complaining about the actual change, tell them how you feel overwhelmed and why, so that they can try to help you instead of just commiserating about your problems.)

- **Manage technology.** Learning about updates and new programs can be frustrating. However, it should only take a few weeks, and the changes will iron themselves out and integrate into your new routine in no time.

- **Make time for leisure.** It's important to take a break from work. Even if you have to take work home with you once in a while, take time out every day to do something meaningful to you. Burning out on too much work is not an option.

Quality of work-life and work/life balance has to do with how productive you are too. Having healthy work habits will lead you to a stronger sense of career satisfaction and help you manage how you work. If you aren't happy with how your workday goes, know that there are a few ways to change your mindset and actions.

First, figure out why you aren't as productive as you'd like to be. Do you have bad habits? Do you spend all your time reacting to put out fires instead of being proactive? Make a note of everything you think is a bad habit, including things like taking five minutes (which usually turns into twenty minutes) to talk to your coworker about something. What about taking breaks? Do you find yourself taking more time away from your station than doing actual work? Do you check out articles on the internet more than you find yourself working on your documents?

Make sure that you have at least three things to work on. When you do, think of ways that you can reverse your bad habits. I have a few tips that can help you create good habits. Remember, it takes twenty-one days to incorporate a new habit into your routine. If you forget to do something one day or fall back into old habits, don't worry. You can start over and pick it up when you remember.

- **Sleep, sleep well, and sleep enough.** The Director of Boston University's Center for Psychological Rehabilitation department, Dr. William A. Anthony, found that 70 percent of Americans admitted to sleeping on the job. These people were not lazy; they slept because they needed to sleep. Long work hours, too-early commuting, and overwhelming responsibilities at home have increased the number of people who aren't sleeping. Without sleep, your prefrontal cortex becomes vulnerable, which will affect your work and production! People aged twenty-six to sixty-four should be getting seven to nine hours of sleep a night—if you can't get that in, napping is the ideal way to go for productivity's sake.
- **Find a time when you are at your best, and do the hard stuff then.** If you are bright-eyed and bushy-tailed early in the morning, don't spend your time doing uninspiring tasks. Hit your hardest tasks when you are the most energetic. If you are sluggish after lunch, make sure that easier, repetitive tasks are on your list in the afternoon.
- **Take care of you.** Eat well, drink water often (not coffee, not iced tea, not soft drinks, *water*) and eliminate bad eating and social habits by replacing them with better ones. Be as kind to yourself as you are to others, and steer clear of toxic relationships.

- **Don't worry about multitasking.** As mentioned, multitasking on projects or even on emails will create chaos and confusion for everyone involved. If you are splitting your focus into projects or tasks, it will show. In fact, evidence has been found that multitasking kills productivity. A University of London study showed that when people work on more than one project at one time, their IQ drops fifteen points.Another study found that multitasking can lower gray-matter density in parts of the brain connected to emotional control, decision-making, empathy, and the brain's response to rewards.
- **Give yourself daily to-dos.** At the end of the workday, create a to-do list for the next day. When you get the items out of your head, you're freeing up room for focus on other things that need attention in your personal life, helping you switch from work life to home life and manage stress.
- **Cut your to-do list down.** Getting through your list is a great feeling, but if you have a never-ending list of items that you have to work on, then the point of doing a to-do list becomes superfluous. Instead, limit yourself to a specific number of items each day by breaking the list into categories (daily, weekly, monthly, or urgent/non-urgent). The key here is to work your way up to being more productive. When you are trying to narrow down your projects, ask yourself this: How many items on my to-do list can I realistically complete or make progress on tomorrow, and what are the most important projects on my list?
- **Spruce up your workspace.** Adding a few plants, your favorite colors, and photos organized in a creative way, can make you happy to be at work. Also, adding drawer organizers with color-coded folders is a nice way to organize your space while keeping it focused on how your brain works best.

- **Can you delegate anything?** If you are in a position to delegate, you should do it; chances are you'll like it. Having other people do tasks that you don't have time for will give you a chance to complete more work! Don't forget to check the work that they've done and give them helpful feedback. The last thing you'll want to do is have someone doing something wrong for you but not know it. However, make sure that when you delegate, you're letting your team work with you. There is a very fine line between empowering and micromanaging, and you'll want to make sure that you aren't hovering.

- **Get rid of distractions.** Email notifications, phone calls, and people knocking on your door can get distracting. At the same time, you have to learn to adapt to the noises of your work environment. If you allow yourself to become too distracted, you'll wind up losing precious time. Designate a chunk of time to focus solely on one task and shut out the surrounding chaos. Let your team know you'll be unavailable for a set time, and turn off your phone and email notifications.

- **Use a pending folder.** When you use a pending folder, it helps keep your files in order, your desk manageable, and documents from piling up.

- **If your papers pile up, clean them up.** Schedule a time to go through these documents each week. Having random papers lying about in many places (or even in one place) can continue to overwhelm your mind, which will lead to overstimulation mentally.

- **Schedule your calls.** Giving yourself a management system for important meetings and calls is the best way you know when you are needed and for how long. While there are times when some calls will run over, having an exact time and date on a calendar will give your brain a break from any stress you may feel from worrying about incoming calls.

Collectively, schedule a time when you need to make all outgoing calls as well. This way, you're not constantly reminding yourself later that night about that call you forgot to make while you're trying to sleep.

- **Clear up your workspace once a week.** Take one hour a week and put items back in their place, throw papers away, and reorganize your calendar (if need be). Soon enough, you'll be able to clean your area every day, but remember: start off with small goals.

- **Exercise.** Physical activity can give you immediate benefits. Exercising during the day will give you enhanced brain power that can help you focus, give you more creativity, and allow you to learn faster. Because of the release of dopamine when you work out, you will also find that getting along with others is easier too. In fact, Leeds Metropolitan University found that 65 percent of employees who used the gym at lunchtime had better interactions with their coworkers and became more productive during the latter half of the day.

- **Find your happy place.** When you are more comfortable, you are more productive. Optimistic people have been found to be more successful and effective. While you are at work, when it's easier to be cynical, you have to change your approach; instead of expecting the worst results, try thinking about the best that could happen. If the best results are still a little far-fetched for you, try not having any expectations at all and remind yourself that whatever happens, you'll be fine.

You can change your attitude toward your job if you give yourself the opportunity to take personal and career growth chances. Your company should also offer you ways to learn more about your job and provide you with room to grow into a new role.

Ask yourself: Do you like work that is routine, or do you want to involve your proactivity and creativity in each role? Knowing what kind of employee you are, how you like to work, and what type of problem-solver you can be will help you get to the position you want. This knowledge will give you a better understanding of incorporating work/life balance into the rest of your pillars. Other ideas that can help you learn how to create balance are:

- **Put your foot down**. Realize that you cannot do everything alone. You also don't know everything. Get a mentor, counselor, or join a peer group for help. Make a choice and stick to it to help minimize your emotional distress. The feelings inside of you don't have to stay submerged, and if you let them remain buried, they will begin to fester and create other problems that you will have to deal with in the future. Don't do that to your future self.
- **Learn from your mistakes**. Mistakes happen. New tasks take time to learn and everyone starts out nervous in the beginning. Cut yourself some slack and be patient with

yourself. If you change your mindset, you can put mistakes into an entirely new and healthy perspective. You'll stop beating yourself up and start asking yourself, *What can I learn here?* You will become more efficient and confident at tasks set with repetition.

- **Manage your goals.** One motivational quote I see frequently is "Shoot for the moon. Even if you miss, you'll land among the stars." While it sounds like a good idea on the surface, don't set your goals so high that you can't reach them. When you do that, you're only setting yourself up for failure. Instead, know what your limits are, know what you can do, and know when and where you can push your limits. Create a list of things to do, prioritize them, and get rid of the tasks that aren't needed.

- **Use your time wisely.** Procrastination is a huge contributor to stress. Normally, if you put something off because you don't want to do it, you'll put it off again, and a third time, and then you are up until four in the morning on deadline day scrambling to finish it. Even if you do get finished with the task, you'll probably find your work is lacking. If the project seems too daunting, break it up into smaller pieces and complete one part at a time. Remember to take a step back and have a break, but make it no more than fifteen minutes, otherwise you might get dragged into something else or distracted by workplace conversations.

- **Be flexible.** If your work allows it, ask for some time away from the office. Do your work in an environment where you can focus completely on the project at hand.

- **Break time!** A study conducted at Cornell University in the Ergonomics department found that the key to productivity is to build movement into your daily routine:

Sit to do computer work. Sit using a height-adjustable, downward-tilting keyboard tray for the best work posture, then every twenty minutes, stand for eight minutes **AND MOVE** for two minutes. The absolute time isn't critical, but about every twenty to thirty minutes, take a posture break and stand and move for a couple of minutes. Simply standing is insufficient. Movement is important to get blood circulation through the muscles. And movement is **FREE**! Research shows that you don't need to do vigorous exercise (e.g., jumping jacks) to get the benefits; just walking around is sufficient. So build in a pattern of creating greater movement variety in the workplace (e.g., walk to a printer or water fountain, stand for a meeting, take the stairs, walk around the floor, and park a bit further away from the building each day).

- **Communicate!** Let your team know when you are overwhelmed, need help, or feel pushed against the wall. Chances are you're not the only one feeling this way. Other people might be feeling the crunch too. Don't tell your team every minor detail about your life, but if things are rough for you, don't pretend like everything is under control. A lot of people are intuitive and can tell when things aren't going to plan. Be brave enough to say, *This isn't working for me*, and develop a new way to do it.

If you are going to start to get balance in your life, work is one of the biggest places to begin. Like with your home pillar, it may not happen all at once, and you may have to take small breaks in or around each step, but slowly adding them into your daily routine will have you seeing things in a new light faster than you realize.

Your "Work" Steps

Typically, your workplace is where you spend a good chunk of your week. If your workspace is cluttered and you are in a constant battle with yourself to either leave work because nothing seems to get done, or work well into the night at the office, chances are your work pillar is far from balanced.

Assess Your Work Life

The first step you'll take will be to assess your work life. Does your workspace reflect a clean and clutter-free environment? Do you meet deadlines? Do you wake up in the middle of the night with lists of things you have to do running through your head for the next day? Are you comfortable in the environment you work in? Are you working for just a paycheck, or do you like your job? Do you like the people you work with?

Answering these questions will give you insight into how you view work. There is an enormous surge of people looking for jobs that make them happy, environments that treat them well, and treat them as more than just a number. If you're not happy with what you do, if you find your work life has toxicity and you want to get rid of it, or if you aren't satisfied with the pay you make, it's time to set some new goals for yourself.

On the other hand, if you really love your job but find yourself constantly at work with no time for anything else, it's time to look hard at what you really want.

Evaluate What You Want

This evaluation is going to be very similar to the home pillar. We will need to utilize a list in our journals or a vision board of goals we want to meet. Consider asking yourself what you want to improve on in your work life:

- Is your work environment cluttered?
- Do you want new opportunities?
- Are you late for work or unable to meet deadlines?
- Do you want to connect more with coworkers?
- Are you satisfied with your job? What do you want to change?

Getting these thoughts down will help you see where you are lacking, where you are thriving, and what your goals are for your career. If you want to be a manager someday and you work at a retail store, then you know you have a long way to go. If you work for a company with a toxic environment but love the work you do, maybe you can start researching other companies and their cultures. You could make a goal to work for a company where the culture is better.

Start Planning

Once your goals are in place, you can start planning how you're going to get there. What you need to do now is start setting deadlines. These deadlines will guide your next actions and won't all have the same timeframes. I suggest using a journal with a list and a calendar to map out your plans.

If you want to clean up your work area, that should be a simple task that could take a few hours. So the deadline could be "by the end of the week," or "at the end of the month, my work area will be clean and organized." Make sure cleaning out your digital footprint is included. An inbox with 12,000 emails is not an organized inbox, and just looking at that is sure to stress you out!

If you are hoping to complete a project by a specific deadline, that will take more planning. Break down your task into smaller parts. See how many pieces will contribute to a completed project and schedule deadlines to meet each part of the project. The idea is a ladder effect. Once you finish one rung, you move on to the next, and sooner than you notice, you'll be at the top of the ladder and your project will be done.

You will want to give yourself some cushion for mistakes and fixes as well. No project is perfect, but don't stress about the issues because each time a new problem arises it will give you a chance to learn something new.

Lastly, if you want a promotion or a job change, plan out how to get there. If you are looking for a new job, it's best to start with research. Research the market you want to work in, find out what they are paying, and talk to some people in that field.

Similarly, if you want a promotion within your company, start putting your feelers out, reach out to someone who was interviewed for the position you want or has a similar position as you do right now. You can get your foot in the door by simply asking a few questions over a coffee, but if you want to keep moving up the career ladder, reach out to find some mentors. If your company does not have a mentor program, then suggest that they get one or create one on your own. Creating programs and initiatives within your company culture is a great way to get your name out to the higher-ups; you can also meet some fascinating people you may never have met before.

Take Action

Once your plans are laid out, it's time to put them into motion. Deadlines will be looming over you; try not to focus on the far-out ones. Instead, take the first step by completing the closest date. There will be some things that may not fit into your work schedule due to projects and other deadlines. However, if you want a clean work area—and that is your first goal—make time to get it done.

This may take you coming in early or staying late a few nights to ensure that the goal is met, but once your workspace (including your digital workspace) is clean, it will be easier to clean up as you go from that moment on.

If your workspace is cleared away, people will recognize it. Your clean desk can inspire others to be organized as well—or if you are looking for a promotion, having your space clutter-free is a great way to get noticed and start a conversation about it.

If your goal is a new job, make time for job hunting before or after work. It's important to note that you *should never job hunt at work or on a work computer*. It might seem obvious, but if your supervisor walks by and looks over your shoulder to see you researching other jobs when you should be working, it isn't going to reflect well on you in any capacity. Use the internet to your advantage: a lot of companies don't offer paper applications or require that you apply online, and there are a huge number of job-hunting websites that can help you get the information that you need and put you in contact with companies looking to hire new workers.

Remember when you look at other jobs to look at more than just the hourly pay or salary. You want to know about healthcare, benefits, commute time, location, company hierarchy and where you will fit into it, what the actual work entails, and the reputation of the company you're looking at compared to your current employment situation. This is all the bare minimum of what you should be looking at before you even apply for a job you like. You will have to weigh up what is important to you in this respect, and there are plenty of available resources that can help you weigh up the pros and cons of the job compared to your current one and help you put together a good-looking resume to apply for it.

If you find a job that you like, don't procrastinate getting your resume and application in order. Make time before or after work to get it ready and send it in as soon as possible, and make sure to look out for any communication from your point of contact. If they offer you an interview and you can work out a time to meet up for it, take time off work to get prepared for it if you need to. There are resources available to use to help you determine what you need to wear, how to behave, and what kind of questions to ask of your interviewer. Once you're finished with the interview and you have the information that you need, provide follow-up communication with the interviewer that same day, either by way of a phone call or an email, thanking them for their time and either confirming your interest in the job or declining further interest. Time is of the essence on something like this because there's always a chance that someone could be offered the same position and snatch it up before you even find the email offering you the job.

Reassess Your Progress

Assessing your plan and progress for work is pretty similar to evaluating your home life. There are a few questions you'll have to ask yourself at the end of the week:

1. Are you making your deadlines?
2. Are you keeping your work area clean?
3. Are you finding good information from your research?
4. Do you have new goals you want to reach?

5. What can you do better?
6. Where are you doing well?

If you find that you have some good momentum, keep going! If you find that you're lacking in certain areas, make sure to pick up the pace and try to see if changing your planning steps can help you make improvements.

Are you meeting new people for you to get promoted? Are you keeping your work area clean despite the busy schedule you have? Are you making time to job hunt if you need to? If your job hunt isn't going so well, do you have something that is lacking in appeal and is it something you can change?

If your answer is no, make sure to tweak your plan or revisit your goals. If it is yes, understand that you will always have ways to improve your work, so it's a good idea to review the plans you wrote to see if there are places where you can hone your methods.

Just because you spend a large chunk of your time working doesn't mean that work is the only thing you do. That being said, know that an organized and clutter-free work life helps you take a step away from work. Knowing your work goals will also give you a chance to unwind outside of work. Everything in the work pillar will grant you an opportunity to relax and better manage yourself, which can help you be more productive at work and help you go farther in your career. It can also help you assess where you are in your job and see if you need to plan to get a new one.

5

MONEY DOESN'T BUY HAPPINESS, BUT IT DOES HELP!

"You'll never get organized if you don't have a vision for your life."

LINDA EUBANKS

CORA HAS her life figured out to a T . . . well, mostly.

At thirty-three, she has a full-time job, exercises daily, makes time for her friends, and her apartment is organized. She becomes overwhelmed when she thinks of money. So, instead of paying her bills on time she avoids her money problems by simply adding her bills to a pile on her desk. She lives paycheck to paycheck and that's all she's known, but she doesn't want to rent forever. She knows the next step will be to buy a starter home, but she's never really planned for something so large before. Saving money for a down payment seems unachievable right now, but she is serious about wanting a house. She is ready for the next step in her life and she wants to see how long it would take to make a financial plan and develop good habits with her money.

After briefly looking at her finances, Cora sees that not only does she not have a plan in action, but if an emergency popped up, she would not have the ability to support herself. Don't even think about bringing up starting a retirement plan or saving for her future! She knows she should start saving for retirement and has heard it from everyone, from her coworkers to the mailman. Everywhere she turns, someone is talking about money, and even though she talks herself into sitting down and writing out a budget to get herself on track, she manages to distract herself with anything else she can get ahold of.

Life keeps moving forward while Cora's money anxiety grows, bills fall behind, and she steps closer toward her future each day. Without proper intervention, Cora will wake up one day and have no way to take care of herself.

Money is stressful for many people. Between juggling debt, day-to-day purchases, savings, and impulse buying, putting a budget together can be difficult.

Having a balanced financial life will give you room to breathe when there is an emergency; it will mean not living paycheck to paycheck and having the ability to put away money for savings and splurge a little on yourself, guilt-free. If you are financially stable, the idea of paying bills will not burn you out; instead, you'll have a chance to pay your bills early or on time without worrying when the next check will clear.

Balancing your finances will give you the freedom to provide for yourself and your family without staying up at night worrying about how on earth you're going to pay for the next crisis in your household.

What Are Your Financial Goals?

Thinking about finances may not be the ideal way to spend a few hours, but it is crucial. If you want to buy property, provide for your children's future, or retire comfortably later in life, it's important to know what your goals are now. Think of all those commercials that tell you "it's never too early to start thinking about retirement." Starting off with a few small goals and building up to end goals is going to be the way to manage this idea. At first, you can have a goal of saving $500, which will then move up to paying off all credit card debt, and have an end goal of keeping $20,000 in savings for emergencies. Depending on your pay rate, scale, and pay schedule, you can work on more than one of these goals at a time, but keep your ideas based in reality and aim higher after you have your goals situated.

I've found there are a couple of main sticking points where people go wrong with money. We are going to start with these. Once you straighten these out, you'll find more success with your money.

Budgeting

It's time to get into the mindset where you research and confirm the price of something before you assume you can or can't afford it. This idea will give you an opportunity to use your budget and balance your checking account to help you make decisions on big purchases, emergencies, and day-to-day expenses.

Without having your finances in check, you may be left stranded when an emergency occurs and planning for the future will not be possible. On average, only 17 percent of people say they feel they will be ready for retirement. That means six out of ten people have no financial cushion or very little money ready for when they need to retire. Don't let yourself be one of them.

When you have money in your account, that doesn't mean you should use it. There are things that you need the money for and expenses that you have to consider. If you've never had luck managing a budget or never tried making one, pulling a shiny new budget out of thin air can be tricky.

One easy way to get started is to look for an online budget template. Giving yourself a template to work from can help you understand what kind of items to put on your budget. There are many online resources that can help you tailor your needs and give you ideas for your own personalized planner. One of the most common budgets is the 50/30/20 method.

The 50/30/20 method was popularized by Elizabeth Warren and her daughter. The rule uses your income after tax and separates your money into three areas. With this method you will put 50 percent of your money into the "needs" area, 30 percent will go into your "wants" area, and 20 percent goes into your "financial goals."

The "needs" area are items you cannot live without, like clothes, food, mortgage or rent, and utilities. Your "wants" money can be used for eating out, activities, streaming services, hobbies, and vacations. Your "financial goals" should include any savings you have stored away (or want to have) plus paying off any debts.

When you use the 50/30/20 method you will calculate your monthly income and your spending threshold. Then you will plan your budget with your financial numbers. You will multiply each number separately by your monthly income.

It will look something like this:

Monthly income × 0.5 = budget for needs

Monthly income × 0.3 = budget for wants

Monthly income × 0.2 = budget for financial goals

Once you get your numbers, you plan your budget with them. Each area will have a specific amount you need to spend, and once you tally your expenses match it up with how you actually spend your money. Do you see a difference? Do you see a place where you can improve?

The next step is to track what you spend. When you get coffee once a day at that little coffee shop, chances are you are spending three to six dollars daily, which adds up quicker than you may realize. The little purchases will get you to overspend on your budget. Once a week, gather all your receipts (digital or paper) and add up what you are spending. This action can help you see what you are spending each week and can give you a chance to make sure you're sticking to your budget.

From there, you can build your budget. Listing expenses can seem overwhelming. Adding the numbers up can add to your stress at first, but once you input your expenses and produce your list to see how much money you need to have to live on each month, you'll see that it's not as scary as you thought. If you think that doing a budget will be boring, you can find a way to reward yourself for sitting down and working through it. Budgeting is your best first step, and it's one that's frequently overlooked. Budgeting at the end of each month will bring you less stress and give you a chance to live within your means without worrying about making ends meet.

Once you create your budget, you have to use it, otherwise it's pointless. For the first few months, you should get in the habit of checking it at least once a week to make sure you are on track. After you know more about what you can and can't afford, you may find yourself checking it less often. If you do go over budget, you'll have to figure out how and where to pull the extra money from throughout the rest of the month. Being cautious with your budget is a good idea until you get the hang of it. Doing this will help you feel like you have a bit of financial freedom, even if it is treating yourself to an ice cream at the end of the week. Make sure that you *save* the rest of the money not allotted to your expenses or unbudgeted limit; if you do, you can come up with a nice cushion in your checking account.

With your new budget, you can put it into action and the best way to keep up with it is to continue the routine of checking your monthly payments against what you are actually making. You can keep doing this until you are comfortable with your budget, but make sure it's part of your pillar maintenance as well. Soon enough, it will become second-nature and you'll be planning out your budget for years in advance instead of just one month at a time.

Other methods that are similar to the 50/30/20 method include the 80/20 (expenses/savings) rule or the 70/20/10 (spending/savings/debt) rule; both of these methods give a little more wiggle room for those who are starting a new job or recently graduated college.

Remember that your money practices may not be solid when you first begin, or you may keep up with the budget for the first couple of months before you lose steam. If you catch yourself getting a little too relaxed with your spending or you stop checking your budget each month, you have to get back into the habit. Self-discipline is the best way to make sure this works for you.

Finally, learn to accept your debt. Not all debt is bad. Although there are times when it seems that owing a continuous monthly payment stretches your dollar, payments like home loans can actually be productive for your financial management. Accept your debt and divide it into two categories: productive and nonproductive. Mortgage payments will help you build equity, which increases your net worth. Credit card debt can be viewed as unproductive because it won't add to your net worth or enhance your financial future.

Once you've gotten your debt categorized, make your unproductive debt central to your financial goals. Eliminate that as quickly as you can by paying it off or refinancing, especially if that debt has higher interest rates.

And remember to always save some of your money. You are going to have to make some big purchases in your life. You cannot get around it, so avoiding impulse purchases and putting off larger investments where you can is going to help you out long-term. If you are looking to buy a new television, phone, or computer, put a little money away each week to buy it and don't take out a new credit card to get it. When you save up the money to buy a bigger item, you'll eliminate the need for adding another monthly payment to your budget. Also, along with saving your money for a big purchase, try to contribute money to your savings account once a month. Doing this will help you build healthier financial habits and will encourage more balance in your money life.

You'll also want to get your emergency fund ready. Emergencies happen. Unexpected home repairs, emergency doctor's visits, and car breakdowns can all make the best financial goals fail under pressure. Putting together an emergency fund can be a way to plan for disasters. This fund can be defined in your financial goals and the general rule is to have six months' worth of net household income in a special savings place. This requires discipline because you don't want to use this fund to pay for day-to-day expenses, your impulse buys, or funding your coffee addiction. It's definitely a long-term goal and you don't have to put all your pay into the savings at one time. It's a slow build: as long as you're putting money in, you'll be saving it. Consider shopping around for a savings account with a higher interest rate to help you build up your emergency fund quicker. These types of accounts usually have a monthly limit or a minimum withdrawal fee, so make sure to look at the fine print as well.

Rainy Day Funds

There is an adage about saving money for a rainy day. You still hear it used today because everyone needs to have a nice time once in a while. If you plan your budget and have a little left over each month, save it for yourself. It doesn't have to be a lot, it can be as little as twenty dollars a month. There will come a time when you are grateful to have a little bit saved up to go out with your friends or treat yourself to the movies.

However, not everyone sees their rainy day fund as money to play with. Instead, they use it as an emergency fund. If you are using your budget correctly and keeping up its maintenance, you will end up with a small amount of money left. As long as you stay within your means, you can put a small amount away with each pay.

Of course, if you find that you are living within your means but you are still not making out well enough, you may want to check some things that could be eating away at your finances that you may not even notice. This includes:

- Monthly payments that reoccur without your notice.
- Subscriptions to magazines, streaming platforms, and monthly products.
- Daily coffee purchases, take-out delivery charges, and other convenience fees.
- Late fees.
- Credit card interest.
- Unknown bank fees.

There are, of course, ways to stop having your money soak up into these items:

- **Don't add any more recurring bills to your account.** Recurring monthly bills seem like they are a good idea, and sometimes they are. You have to live somewhere, so you have to pay rent or a mortgage. However, just because you qualify for a loan doesn't mean you should take it. The mail you get and the notifications you see from banks and creditors are based on your income, not what you owe monthly, so adding another loan or monthly payment to your budget will make your numbers shrink. Unless there is an emergency, stay away from making any big purchases or large financial decisions.
- **Pay the best price.** Research your products and pay attention to sales, discounts, and alternatives you could use. You don't always have to shop brand names; the title doesn't mean something is better for you, only that it's more familiar. Like a budget, this step is necessary for finding financial balance.
- **Use credit cards sparingly.** Do you find yourself using credit cards more often than using cash? Even when you have money in the bank, when you constantly charge a card you may not be keeping track of how much you spend, and your credit card bill will skyrocket faster than you realize.

If you are looking to improve your money management, you will have to regularly evaluate your financial goals and keep a close eye on your budget. This practice will require you to form a new habit of keeping receipts and checking your plans to know what is going on with your finances.

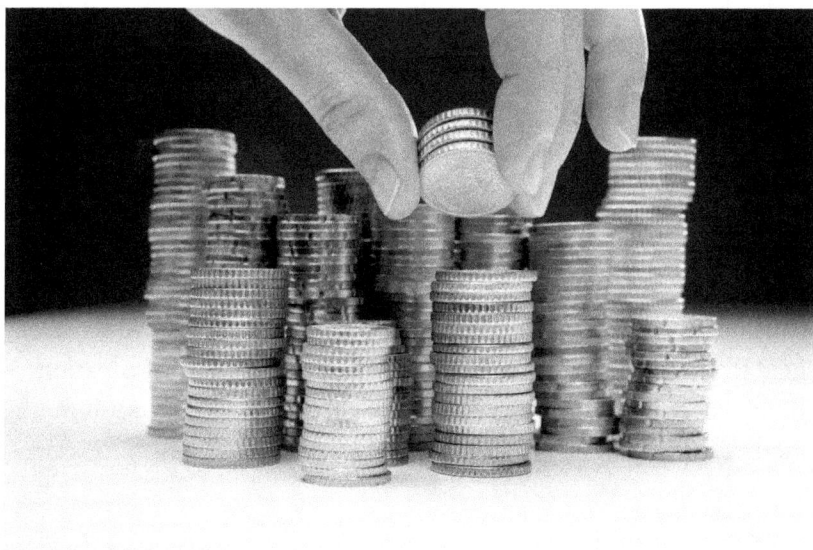

Your "Money" Steps

Assess Your Money Pillar

When you look at your finances, ask yourself how you manage your finances currently. Do you even have a budget? If you don't, then it's time to start one! If you do have one, what does your current budget look like? What method are you using? How is your budget working? Are you still stressed out with your current budget?

Think about how much of a paper trail you've collected throughout the years! *Forbes* has a great list of how long to keep those documents that have been cluttering up your files, desktop, and other spaces. Here is a brief overview:

- Tax records: Seven years.
- Bank and Credit Card statements: One year.
- Insurance claims and warranty documents: Less than a year.

Forbes also cautions that there are documents you should keep forever, such as birth certificates, social security cards, marriage certificates, adoption papers, death certificates, passports, wills and living wills, powers of attorney, legal filings, military records, retirement and pension plans, inheritance documents, and beneficiary forms.

Everything else not mentioned in the section above, should be considered based on your personal needs and then *shredded*. Don't just throw things in the trash with your personal information on them—people go through the garbage specifically to acquire this kind of information!

Evaluate What You Want

If you feel that your money is always tight or that you have no wiggle room, it may be time to revisit your budget for some changes.

If you don't have a budget in place, it's time to do a little research. Start off with the 50/30/20 method as a base. If you're not sure how to outline the budget, research online to find a planner that you like. Set goals and ask yourself some questions:

- What do I want to save money for?
- Do I have savings for an emergency fund?
- Do I have physical financial clutter that needs to be organized?
- Do I have debts that need to be prioritized?
- Do I have a set monetary goal for savings each month?

The goals you lay out will ultimately vary based on your lifestyle, but you need to have a plan so that you don't find yourself asking, *What was I saving for again?* and end up right back to the same place you were before.

Set Your Plan

Outline and use the budget for one month. If you're a pen-and-paper person, there are budget spreadsheets available for you to make or print so that you can write down all your numbers. If you're a digital person and you don't mind the computer doing it for you, there are also budget sheets that will break down the numbers you enter into needs, wants, and savings that you can edit and save. It helps to write your goals at the top or bottom of the budget sheet so that every time you look at the budget, it encourages you to keep working toward your goals.

Take Action

With your plan set, make a date to start implementing and tracking your budget on your chosen calendar. For end of the week evaluations, it may help to start on the first of the next month so that you can evaluate yourself on day seven, fourteen, twenty-one, and twenty-eight of that month. If you are not paid on a weekly basis, you should still do weekly evaluations so that you can see what you spent each week. After a month of budgeting you will know if your plan needs to be tweaked or if it works well.

Remember, with the 50/30/20 method, delegate 50 percent to your needs, 30 percent to your wants, and 20 percent to your financial goals. Stick to the budget for one month. Again, I have to hammer home the need for honesty and self-discipline. Whenever you have the urge to impulse buy a cute throw rug for your home or buy fast food for lunch, stop and ask yourself, *Do I really want this?* because it has to come out of your wants section and you have to get the money from somewhere.

If you run over on your wants, it has to come out of your 20 percent for savings, which will set back the goals you were hoping to achieve. You cannot compromise on your needs easily because of the lack of flexibility. You need food to survive, you need to pay bills to have a roof over your head, and other expenses need to be paid for in order to maintain your standard of living. If you compromise here, this will leave you in a bind when your bills come due, and finding how to come up with the funds when you spent them all on something you did not need is stress that you should not have to deal with when you have a budget.

Reassess Your Progress

Remember to look at those goals at the end of each week when you evaluate your budget and ask if you stayed within your spending limits. If you dipped into your 20 percent savings, be honest and ask yourself if this was due to your lack of self-control or if there really, truly was something that was outside your control that resulted in you needing to spend more than you'd originally hoped. If self-control is the problem, find ways to limit yourself, consider asking a family member to help you monitor what you purchase, only carry two methods of payment on you at all times, and keep your credit cards and debit cards out of easy reach to keep your impulse buying in check.

After your first month, look at the progress you are making. Is the budget you set out working? Did an emergency strike? Did you have enough money saved away to pay for it? If you were ready for the emergency and things seemed to work out, then keep going with your budget. If you find that you need to fix some things, reassess and rearrange to meet your goals.

6

ME, MYSELF, AND MY SMARTPHONE

"Clutter is not just physical stuff. It's old ideas, toxic relationships, and bad habits. Clutter is anything that does not support your better self."

ELEANOR BROWN

TEEGAN THOUGHT MOVING to college was going to be different. She thought she was ready for college life, and she thought she was prepared to be out on her own. She's an adult now, she can handle it. It's three months into freshman year and keeping up with her routine is beyond difficult with her classes, hanging out with her friends, and college parties. Her classes are hard, and she has a mountain of homework to complete daily. She misses her mom and dad, even her little sister. She is overworked at her part-time fast-food gig and cannot keep up with cleaning her side of the dorm room. Most of the time, she just throws the next pile of dirty things under her bed and hopes that her neat-freak of a roommate will stop harping on her.

She can't wake up on time, she misses her family, and her roommate constantly makes her feel bad about herself because she seems to be having a smoother transition to college life. The roommate is making friends easily, she has a *constant level of organization on her side of the room, and she doesn't ever seem to be late for anything. Teegan lies in bed at night on her phone trying to list out her homework, due dates, work schedule, find time to see her family, clean her side of the room, and so much else. Then, she wakes up late for class and the cycle starts over again. She feels inadequate, but she doesn't know where to start. The chaos of everyday life has her worried that she will not make it out of the first year of college.*

Why are humans such social creatures? Since it is widely theorized that humans evolved from an extinct subspecies of primate, you don't have to look very far to find examples of primate socialization. All primates, from gorillas and chimpanzees to monkeys and lemurs, live best in small family groups with a wide range of social interactions. They chatter and communicate, they fight and make up, they groom and feed each other, and they take care of each other's young.

While humans have a different range of social interactions, for the most part we are not so different in this regard. Being social was a survival strength when our ancestors switched from foraging for food at night to doing more activities throughout the day. As humans evolved, they wanted to share more ideas, so they developed a basic form of communicating with each other. Throughout this time, researchers found that our species held an innate compassion. This empathy served especially well when a human went looking for a partner. Social and compassionate humans found more success within their group hierarchy and in attracting a partner, which helped to grow the species. In turn, babies looked after by compassionate parents learned this behavior from them, which further encouraged its emergence.

Humans are so social that they developed the tools needed to keep communication flowing even when our friends or family move across the world. While forms of communication started off small through smoke signals, flags and banners, and written letters, they quickly transformed into telegrams, telephone calls, and the internet.

Like other primates, humans are gregarious and live in family units. Humans are born into a family and surrounded by parents, adults, and loved ones. These people guide and help us throughout our lives. If it is not a parent, another adult will be in charge of your upbringing, and you will interact with an untold number of people within your lifetime. Not all the interactions will be positive—you may fight with your family, with your coworkers, your bosses, or your friends. Despite that, whether you are an extrovert or an introvert, humans still need to be around humans, for better or worse.

Once you step into adulthood, you may find that you avoid social situations with other people due to a chaotic home life, work burnout, financial hardships, and overwhelming health obligations taking up all your time, which may cause your social pillar to suffer. People generally appreciate shared experiences, while even more people enjoy the positivity and encouragement from friends that keep pursuing healthy activities and trying new things. Mainly, people can help you put things into perspective and give you a chance to destress. A healthy support system is vital to our success and growth as human beings.

When we are around people, there is a part of our brain that releases a cocktail of neurotransmitters. The release of these chemicals helps to regulate our response to stress and anxiety. In fact, psychologist Susan Pinker has described face-to-face contact as a vaccine for our brains:

> Face-to-face contact releases a whole cascade of neurotransmitters, and, like a vaccine, they protect you now, in the present, and well into the future, so simply [...] shaking hands, giving somebody a high-five is enough to release oxytocin, which increases your level of trust and it lowers your cortisol levels, so it lowers your stress.

Besides the in-person brain kick we get, we are also motivated by social interactions and it gives way to even more kinds of brain power. Research has found that when interacting with other people, we train our brains to improve memory and recall. Evidence shows that social interaction protects the brain from neurodegenerative diseases as well.

Social context is also important. Recent studies have shown that having social connection increases health benefits by allowing humans to form better habits and live a healthier life. Alternatively, those who are not as social had a 60 percent chance of developing prediabetes, which can form into type 2 diabetes if not monitored.

With the release of beneficial hormones into our brain, it can be said that social interaction is important to living a healthy and well-balanced life. What happens when we neglect interacting with friends and loved ones, and gloss over meeting new people? Your stress levels will go up, your memory and recall will start to go down, and your hopes for a healthy lifestyle can decrease as well.

There are a lot of ways to distract yourself from being in a healthy social setting, and social media is one of them. Even with "social" in the title, we get too sucked into scrolling through our preferred platform, reading negative content, and looking at a filtered "perfect" world, and we don't actually end up productively interacting with anyone on a personal level. When you're on a constant loop of social media, you are lying to yourself if you say that you are still connected with people: you may be connected with the platform, but the people part of social media was lost a long time ago.

Social Media and Clutter

Social connections have a huge impact on our mental health. When we are socially connected, it can reduce anxiety, boost self-worth, relieve stress, and alleviate depression. However, there is worth and value to belonging to a group of people who promote your mental health; the same applies if you are surrounded by unhealthy people.

While there are good points to social media, if you are too focused on seeing who commented on your last post or getting more friends, chances are you're searching for something, but you won't find it solely online.

Social media has become a replacement for in-person relationships. People find a way to connect, but it doesn't replace the need for physical interactions. In-person interactions trigger hormones that encourage stress reduction and a healthier attitude, while the dopamine triggered from getting a "like" or someone using a smiley face emoticon for your post only lasts for a short burst.

When using a computer or smartphone too long in search of that small dose of instant gratification, you wind up feeling anxious, stressed, and isolated. Social media has been linked to self-harm, suicidal thoughts, anxiety, depression, and loneliness, which come from getting a rapid-fire release of dopamine when something small happens.

Harvard University published an article on dopamine levels and the use of social media. Within that article, the authors show the "vicious cycle of unhealthy social media use," which looks a little something like this:

1. You feel anxious, depressed, lonely, or stressed, and you jump online. This reduces your boredom and helps you feel connected to other people.
2. You start to feel a fear of missing out (FOMO). When you do miss out on something, you begin to feel dissatisfaction with your life, so you go online more often.
3. You can't be online 24/7, so your mood will begin to worsen, and your stress levels will start to heighten.
4. You begin to use social media even more to avoid the stress and the isolation you feel, but the short bursts of dopamine are smaller and smaller . . . and your downward spiral continues.

You may find you're distracted in daily life, neglecting in-person relationships, or you walk away feeling angry, depressed, or envious. In that case, chances are you aren't using social media in balance with the rest of your life. Other health and mental health hazards include insomnia or other sleep issues and a lack of self-reflection. Consider the following to regain control from social media:

- Only use your laptop or computer to check social media. Take all unnecessary apps off your phone.

- Consider how many social media apps you *really* need. Are you wasting more time than necessary juggling all the apps in your life?
- Use an app to track time spent on social media platforms. (It might seem counterintuitive since I just said, *Consider how many apps you* really *need*, but this one has a specific purpose —monitoring how you spend your time instead of siphoning your time away!)
- Only let yourself check your phone every two hours instead of every couple of minutes.
- Reduce your time online. Set a goal for yourself (like thirty minutes a day) that will limit your exposure to social media platforms.
- Remember, perfection is unattainable. What you see online is generally a carefully crafted illusion. Subscribe to only positive, wholesome content to keep you grounded within the realm of reality. In the age of digital altering, it's challenging to separate fact from fiction. Phone filters quickly and efficiently alter faces and bodies, videos can be edited, and photos can be angled for a distorted view of the world. Looking at everyone else's "perfect" life will have you seeking something that is unrealistic, leaving you depressed and dissatisfied.
- No matter what you see other people doing, don't just post your first thought. While emotions are not bad in and of themselves, posting something because you are overly emotional and need to get it out will have you regretting what you wrote. Even if you delete it, that message was out there for the world to see at least for a little while, and it's still stored on the platform's server *even if you deleted it*. Avoid getting into arguments with people and don't post emotionally. As a rule, take ten minutes to calm down before you post anything to make sure you are in a rational mindset.

- Use social media with a specific purpose in mind: for business, school, or to keep in touch with real life friends and family. Resolve to use the online platforms in a positive way. Otherwise, stay away from them.
- Turn off your phone for important moments like visiting your family, friends, or engaging in a work activity that needs your full attention (you can also do this several times a day to unwind).
- Disable notifications from social media in your settings (you should do this for any social media platform that gives you the option, and if you have a device that lets you disable social media alerts, use it to your advantage) and set your phone to "nighttime mode" or "do not disturb" during set hours of the day.
- Put your phone on a charger that is not in your bedroom. Charge your phone or tablet throughout the night and give yourself a good amount of sleep.
- Reflect on your day, by yourself, for fifteen minutes or more.
- If you are feeling low or having a bad day, instead of resorting to the comfort of the internet, go for a walk to clear your head or reach out to a friend or family member offline.
- Spend time with the people who are important to you in your real life, not just your social media life! Make time to be with friends, family, or loved ones, join an in-person club, or give back to your community by volunteering.

Following these tips can get you back on a good path for finding balance in your digital life. Starting off by learning how to incorporate one or two of them into your daily life will help you get your life back from the social media monsters.

Making sure that you have a healthy relationship with social media will allow you to assess whether you are feeling stressed, depressed, and anxious or if you are feeling happy, relaxed, and in balance. When you start to use social media sparingly you can make sure that the interactions you do have leave a positive effect on your mood.

Like anything else, social media has both good points and bad points. When you're on an even keel with social media, it augments the friendships you have and lets you communicate with people when they aren't physically close to you. On the other hand, when you're *not* on an even keel with social media, it becomes all-consuming, you find you have no time for anything else, and you spend all day thinking about it, to your detriment. This can happen with dating, too.

Romantic Entanglements

When you start dating a new person, it can be glorious if the person is right for you and you adore them. There are times when the relationship might be all-encompassing and other times when you are so focused on work that the person you are dating becomes an afterthought.

However, you have to balance your dating life with the remainder of your social life and everything else besides. One person doesn't define your whole life, and you certainly shouldn't let them try to! Maybe you aren't looking for a long-term partner right now, or maybe you are just getting back on your feet after a long relationship ended. Maybe you've been hurt in the past and it's a little difficult to open back up again. Regardless of whether the dates go well or not, giving yourself a chance to interact with people you like lets you be more comfortable with yourself as well as with them. Some things you can try are:

1. Remember to keep a good balance between your romantic interests and other obligations. If you are just getting into the swing of things with dating, block off one night a week for date night. However, if you are starting to get into a

deeper relationship, you're going to want to make sure that you are spending quality time with that person, so be thoughtful and include them when you schedule time together.

2. Make time for the truly important people in your life. If there is someone toxic hanging around in your life taking up your valuable time, make it a goal to remove them from your social circle. It just adds to the stress and anxiety with every text or phone call.

3. Remember you should be true to yourself and be truthful *about* yourself. Fabricating your online persona to attract someone's interest will only lead to heartbreak and embarrassment. Don't get caught up in what you feel is expected of you. If what is expected isn't something that you like, there's no shame in admitting that.

4. Be cautious about online dating, especially if it becomes offline dating. If you are meeting someone online for the first time, don't divulge too much personal information like where you live or work. While you liked interacting with them online, you may find that after meeting them in-person they are not someone you want in your life. You might come to regret sharing too much with them.

5. Make the most of your schedule. Lunchtime at work is a great way to get to know someone and give you a chance to have a quick conversation or just spend a few moments with someone you like. A quick call, text, or coffee date to break up the day will leave you refreshed and more fulfilled.

6. Friends and family are equally important, so don't make room just for romance. Finding a balance with friends, family, and romantic interests are an important step to unlocking your social freedom. Schedule time throughout your week to make all those important life events, and do not be afraid to let someone know if something comes up and you need to change plans.

Friends Have Benefits

Dating isn't the only thing, of course. A good friend is priceless: you can talk to them about anything that's on your mind, you can laugh with them and have fun together, and you have a shoulder to cry on or someone to complain to when you need to let off some steam. They know they can ask you for the same thing if they need it, and it's this sort of give and take that benefits both people in the friendship, not just one person. Good friends encourage you to be healthy and safe and do what is right for *you* rather than for other people, and if they know you're feeling down or having trouble they can point you in the right direction or give you advice if you need it. Whether you're having an existential crisis or you just want to hang out, being around friends can make you feel better.

A review in 2010 found that people who have healthy friendships have half the risk of dying prematurely from any cause. This study shows that having a strong foundation in your friendships will decrease your risk of stroke, diabetes, and heart attack. On the other hand, socially isolated people are prone to bouts of loneliness, which are linked to different kinds of health issues like cancer, heart disease, substance abuse, and more

Supportive friends can help to lift your mood and boost your self-confidence as well. Everyone doubts themselves sometimes; talking to a friend can help to banish that doubt or help you understand why you feel that way. In a 2015 study, researchers found that high school students who were depressed were twice as likely to recover if their friends were happy. And, if these same teens were around others who had a healthier mood, they were half as likely to develop depression in the first place.

When you are stressed out and talk to a friend, you get a chance to discuss what's on your mind. Even if you don't speak, just being around people you care about and who care about you will help reduce your stress. Harvard Medical School found:

> Scientists are investigating the biological and behavioral factors that account for the health benefits of connecting with others. For example, they've found that it helps relieve harmful levels of stress, which can adversely affect coronary arteries, gut function, insulin regulation, and the immune system. Another line of research suggests that caring behaviors trigger the release of stress-reducing hormones.

With healthy social relationships in balance with the other parts of your life, you will be able to relieve stress and live a healthier life. But what happens if you don't have a strong support group? Chances are some people in your life may not have the healthiest outlook. These are the people you will have to cut ties with; if not physically, at least do so emotionally.

Toxic Relationships

There will always be reasons to keep a person in your life, especially if they have unhealthy habits, but taking a step back from those people will give you a clearer picture of what is *really* going on. There is a distinct difference between a friend who is going through a hard time and is a little sour because of it, and a person who, no matter what you do, is never satisfied. These kinds of people may be miserable, grouchy, or even downright abusive at times. Instead of hearing what the person says, watch what they do. How do their actions correspond with their words? Do you respect this person for what they do and say? Ask yourself if you were to meet your own self while you're with this person, how would you feel meeting them and their friend group for the first time?

If you don't respect the people you are with and find that your personality, habits, or actions change when you're around them, there is a good chance that you're in a toxic relationship. If your relationship is entirely one-sided, or this person is the kind that gossips behind your back, or points their finger at you when something doesn't go their way, that can also be a bad sign. There is a difference between someone lightheartedly poking fun at your accidentally mismatched socks one day and a "friend" finding a new way to insult every outfit you wear every day of the week.

You might find yourself thinking that you don't just want to throw away a "strong" relationship by cutting them out of your life. You may feel guilty and try to make excuses for their behavior instead. Maybe their current behavior toward you just shows themselves in a bad light. These can be simple observations, not judgments. Look at it this way: you're not throwing away a person, you are starting a process of creating healthy distance from their bad behavior. Refusing to meet up, avoiding engaging in harmful content, and blocking them from social media, are all ways to start creating distance. Eventually, the relationship will diminish on its own from lack of contact. They will recenter their focus on continuing their life without you and vice versa.

Taking that first step in distancing yourself will be difficult, but in time you will come to realize the importance of putting your foot down now and own up to the truth you are hiding from: that this person is no good for you. If someone has unhealthy habits that create or bring out ugly traits about yourself, you have to step away from them. You will want to try to see the good in everyone. That's reasonable, but you have to remember that for all the good in people, some people are just not a good fit.

Accept that this person may live a different type of lifestyle that makes you uncomfortable or leaves you feeling unsafe. If someone engages in unhealthy or unpleasant activities and you don't want any part of it, there is nothing wrong with wanting to step away. You cannot unconditionally accept everyone into your life. You don't have to take dramatic action, like telling them how to live their life; you can simply let go of the idea that you will have a long relationship. Letting a relationship fade away can be difficult and sometimes painful, but if you bring out the worst in each other or disapprove of the life they lead, then it's better for you both.

While you are the only person who can evaluate if a relationship is worth keeping, it is important to trust your instincts if something feels off. Let your intuition guide you when it comes to interacting with them. When you become self-aware, you'll start to realize how you feel when someone is around. If you feel at ease with them and you feel like they don't judge you or force their own expectations on you, your gut lets you know that you've found a friend. However, if you have anxiety and an inexplicable sense that something will go wrong, you need to listen to that. Your intuition will not let you down.

If you're unable to connect with your intuition, pay attention to a person's actions and words. Is it a case of do as I say, not as I do? Does the person send out the same message each day? Ask yourself some of the following questions:

1. Do you accept their decisions and actions? Do they have a positive or negative impact?
2. Do you understand and support this person, and do they help and understand you in turn?
3. How does the conversation flow? Do you have to force it? Are there periods of uncomfortable silence?
4. How do you feel when you are together? Is the feeling good, bad, or indifferent?
5. Do you know they care about you? What actions tell you that they do?
6. Why do you have this person in your life? Are you afraid to be alone or without them, or do they have positive qualities that you genuinely like and respect?
7. What do you admire most about them?

Knowing which people are good or bad for you is only half of the battle. Supportive and healthy relationships have to come from both sides. For example, having a group of supportive friends can do wonders for your mental health, but you have to make sure that you are giving as much as you are getting to make the best out of your friendships. Cultivating a relationship or several can help you manage the stress in your life, but it's good to create boundaries, make time to be with them, and actively listen to what they have to say.

Setting Boundaries

When you create boundaries, don't think of it as bricking yourself off from others with a refusal to let people get a look at the real you. Rather, having respectable boundaries gives them a true sense of who you are, what you are passionate about, and your likes and dislikes.

When you create boundaries, you shouldn't wait until someone crosses them; instead, you should communicate well beforehand so that there is no room for misunderstanding. For example, if you *really* don't like surprises, you need to openly and honestly communicate why. They should respect that, and it should not be an issue in the future. Letting people know what your needs are gives them a chance to meet your expectations, instead of falling flat under misunderstandings or assumptions. By truly taking the time to understand your boundaries, you'll also learn the importance of respecting and understanding other people's boundaries as well.

Your "Social" Steps

Assess Your Situation

Look at your social situation and see where there can be improvement. Start by asking yourself some tough questions about your current situation. When it comes to relationships, do you feel you are losing touch with friends and family? Do you find yourself buried in work to avoid getting close to anyone? Are there toxic people in your life? Do you crave more attention? Are you seeking love?

Let's look at social media. Find out what your purpose is when you log in. When it comes to social media, do you log on to check local events happening in your area? Are you checking in with friends and family? Are you seeking attention? Are you lonely? Are you scrolling through people's "perfect lives" while feeling envious of what they have? Are you generally happy after social media use or unsatisfied with what you were viewing?

Evaluate What You Want

Use this time to journal what you are looking for in life, what new experiences you crave, and what you need to improve on or remove. Where can you focus to feel more at peace? For example, if you want to feel more connected to the people in your social circle, schedule time to be out and active with them. Make time for activities together to help strengthen the bond that you share. If you want to meet new people, you have to be prepared to put yourself out there and expand on your hobbies and interests.

Do you want to break free from the hold social media has on your life? Consider the steps needed to scale back your online presence. What is your purpose for logging in to social media? Be cautious about being sucked into the never-ending spiral constantly giving you something new to consume. If you are frustrated by a toxic person, online or offline, ask yourself if you are surrounding yourself with the right people. It might be best to start the process of distancing yourself from them in your life and move on.

If you are seeking love, research the dating apps available to you or consider taking up a hobby you would feel comfortable and confident in to meet new people. If you suffer from social anxiety, research support groups in your area that can help you conquer your fears and meet new people at the same time.

Remember to ask yourself how you fit into the picture as well. Some inner reflection can go a long way here. Do you feel that you could be a better friend? Are you actively there for them and listening to their problems? What can you do better for your children? Have you missed their last two softball games? Do you feel they can talk to you openly about any problems they might have? Is there a roadblock in your relationship? Are you openly communicating the problem and working together as a team to clear it?

I feel it is important to note that trying new things, depending on your anxiety levels, can be downright scary or even debilitating for some. Don't let fear win out! Small steps can lead to big changes in your life. Consider also using this step to do some research in evaluating the options out there. There is a whole world of possibilities to explore!

Plan How to Get Results

Planning out how you are going to achieve these goals is essential for success. Use the internet, your local library, and talk to coworkers, family, and friends to research possibilities to get yourself out there on a new adventure or strengthen bonds you already have in place. Make a list of all the things you want to try, big or small. Research the possibilities to see what is available to you and within your comfort levels and remember to book them into your calendar.

When researching activities, consider what season it is and your geographical location. Are you near the beach in summer? Are there any scenic hiking trails you can try this autumn? Have you always wanted to go ice skating with your significant other? How about a simple hot chocolate meetup at your local coffee shop? Are there attractions in your area you've never visited? Remember to log dates and times and if any reservations are required in advance.

Schedule in time for social media, how long you use it for, and when you need to step away from it. Plan to go through your notifications, delete extra apps and baggage, and make sure to give social media a wide berth before you sleep. If you don't sign out of social media before you go to bed, chances are you'll have a hard time unwinding. Take note that the blue light emitted from your electronic device's screen triggers your brain to stay awake for longer. Your electronic device may have a "nighttime mode" that blocks out blue light, or you can download an app, use blue light glasses, or simply refuse to check your phone at least thirty minutes before bed for better quality sleep.

Removing toxic relationships will take time and planning. Start by distancing yourself from that person by taking time to block them on social media and through other methods of contact. Make it a point to not return requests demanding something of you. Restate boundaries if necessary and focus on filling your life with positive people and content. Your goal here is to create distance and let the relationship fade over time to a level that is acceptable to you. Your goal is not to judge them, instruct them on their life path, or even make up an explanation. Your goal is distancing yourself for a healthier, happier you.

In regards to dating, you can search for online possibilities or in-person. Each app or dating platform is used for specific reasons and you can try out a few for free to find out what ones work best. Otherwise, if you'd prefer to meet people in person, ladies nights at restaurants or bars are still the go-to for most. Library programs, churches, community centers, and other events can all get you meeting people. Find out what there is to do in your area and how it relates to your likes and dislikes.

Take Action

The actual action is always the hard part, but now you can start trying new (or old) things. If you have a group of friends, reach out to them and ask them if they want to go with you. If no one can, then do it yourself; look at it as a chance to possibly meet someone new, or just enjoy being by yourself—there's no shame in some "you" time!

To encourage yourself to be more social, also send a text message weekly to the people you care about the most. Reaching out even by text gives you a chance to reconnect with them or help them feel better about themselves because they know someone is thinking about them.

Taking pictures during your travels and journaling what you like and dislike is all part of the experience. Aim to make it fun and tailored to your needs. Find your preference for documenting your memories.

Don't forget to reward yourself for taking leaps and bounds to make your goals a reality; you are more likely to stick to them if you give yourself some positive reinforcement. Maybe after a night out meeting new people, a relaxing bubble bath is just what you need. Finally got up the courage to remove toxicity from your life? Now *that* sounds deserving of an ice cream sundae and a guilt-free nap!

Reassess Your Progress

Consider assessing your progress weekly to start out. Ask yourself a few questions to see how you're doing. Focus on the successes you've achieved, and hold yourself accountable on the things that did not make the cut. Ask yourself what happened, what went wrong, and how you can do better next week. When you reassess your progress, consider the following:

1. How are you doing so far? Did you try anything new? Did you do anything proactive this week?
2. How are you feeling? Are you pleased with what you've done? Did you like or hate the experience? Why?
3. Did you make any excuses for not achieving a goal you set out? Why?
4. What will your next goal be?

Remember, being honest doesn't mean that you beat yourself up for what you didn't do or were too scared to try. Honesty means that you review what you achieved, look at where you took shortcuts, and give yourself ways to make it better for next time. Hold yourself accountable, but forgive yourself for any mistakes you made. Relationships are a lot more complex than they look. Building that understanding of what went right and wrong is not always apparent at first glance. Don't debase yourself right now because you *didn't* do something. Instead, look at it as an opportunity to do things *better*.

7

HEALTHY BODY, HEALTHY MIND

*"All you need is the plan, the road map, and the courage
to press to your destination."*

EARL NIGHTINGALE

THESE DAYS, Rose is always feeling a bit under the weather. Always feeling tired and lethargic, she makes it a habit to use her lunch break to pick up a large, sugary latte with extra whipped cream from her local coffee shop to combat her drowsiness and keep her going through that afternoon slump. While she's there, she can't help but notice the smell of freshly baked donuts. She just has to have one.s

Rose ends up going home around eight that night after an extended shift at work. She's tired again and her hands are shaking on the wheel. She's already made up her mind that she can't be bothered to make herself a meal when she gets home. She passes another fast-food joint and thinks, Why not, it's too late to cook anyway! *and gets a large order of chicken and fries.*

The next day, she has herself scheduled for a doctor's visit. After discussing possibilities of her continued tiredness and occasional shaking, the doctor's increased concerns sent her on her way for some diagnostics. It turns out at twenty-eight, Rose has diabetes. She knew about the increased risk that runs in her family, but she thought nothing about it considering her age. However, her poor diet choices day in and day out ended up accelerating her illness. The first thing the doctor suggested was to cut down on all things sugary, fun, and tasty. How will she cope now?

Your last pillar, but by no means your least, is your own health. You'll hear it from so many people that you need to take care of yourself to be able to function at your best. It's no secret that taking care of your body with healthy foods and regular exercise gives you more energy to tackle your projects and problems, regardless of what you need to do. Did you also know that emphasis on your health extends past the body and also encompasses the mind? When you eat right and exercise often, your brain will reward you with healthy doses of hormones that will keep your mood elevated, help you feel better, and keep you on a more even keel.

Think of it this way: your body can be compared to a well-oiled machine. If everything is cared for and maintained regularly, the risk of complications and unpleasant breakdowns decreases significantly.

These breakdowns can be physical or mental. When you have headaches, body aches, exhaustion, or digestive upset, these can lead you to have mood swings, increased stress, and even depression.

We can then conclude that simply taking better steps to prevent your bodily "machine" from breaking down can be beneficial to your other pillars. Your home is less chaotic because you have the energy and mindset to efficiently run your household. With your increased energy and mood boost, you have fewer sick days at work and increased job satisfaction. You have better control of your finances because you do not need to spend money on costly and sometimes preventable health conditions, and you have more time and energy to spend with the people that matter most to you.

When was the last time your "machine" went for diagnostics? Regular checkups help prevent illnesses from flying under the radar and potentially becoming unmanageable. Unlike a machine, we cannot replace moving parts as easily, nor can we throw our old bodies away and buy a new one when something goes wrong, so learning to take care of that body is essential. Your body's "technician," in the form of your doctor, can point you in the right direction if you have an underlying condition that has gone unnoticed. These underlying conditions are responsible for more than just bodily breakdown; they could be responsible for mental and behavioral changes as well.

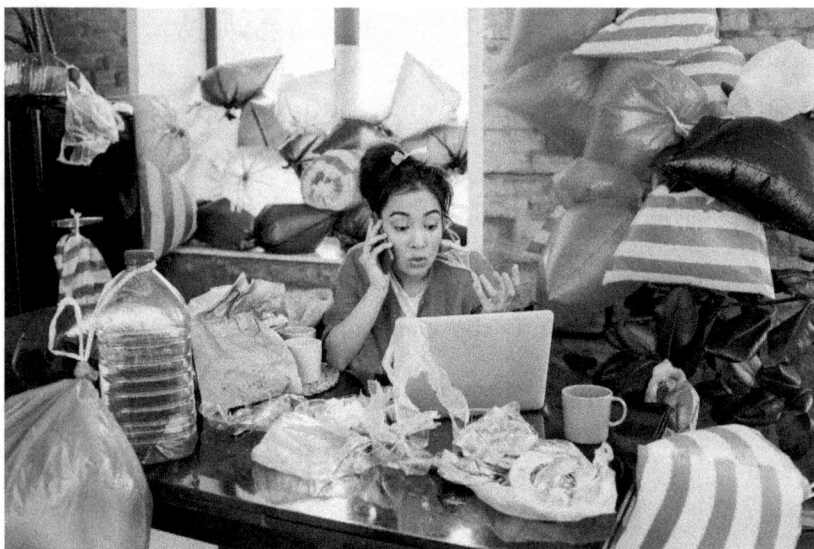

Clutter Can Point to Unknown Health Issues

Earlier we covered the psychology of clutter, and while clutter affects how you feel, it can also be caused by an underlying issue. Attention deficit disorder (ADD), depression, or obsessive-compulsive disorder (OCD) can be a few health issues signaled by excessive amounts of clutter and disorganization. These illnesses can sometimes be debilitating if they aren't dealt with behaviorally.

Chronic Disorganization vs. Hoarding Disorder

Chronic disorganization (CD) and compulsive hoarding disorder (HD) are two different things. While they look the same on the surface, you may not realize that if you are chronically messy, it could be a side effect of ADD, ADHD, a traumatic brain injury (TBI), Alzheimer's disease, or a chronic pain disorder. HD is considered a medical condition on its own.

Hoarding disorder is a diagnosable mental illness with a description that can be found in the DSM V (the *Diagnostic and Statistical Manual of Mental Health Disorders*, Fifth Edition).

Three key characteristics of HD are:

- Failure to throw away or get rid of items that are large in number or size that have no apparent value.
- The prevention of living areas to be used for the room's intended purpose where extreme clutter has piled up.
- Hoarding that causes severe distress or functioning impairment.

These traits also included in the description:

- The inability to ignore purchasing, collecting, or acquiring free items that will only add to your clutter.
- Clutter interferes with your ability to work or go to school, social events, family functions, or if it can pose health and safety risks, bring in the authorities, or cause problems with your neighbors.
- The issue has continued for over six months and is not in line with other mental disorders, medical conditions, or substance abuse.

Chronic Disorganization is usually a hallmark of another issue completely. However, it does have to do with a quality of life issue. If you experience depression or have ADD, ADHD, Alzheimer's disease, or another cognitive functioning issue, know that this issue can be remedied through intervention and help.

Three key characteristics of CD are:

- The inability to get organized for most of your adult life.

- The disorganization negatively affects your daily quality of life.
- Self-help attempts show failure each time you've tried them in the past.

These traits are also recognizable in CD:

- If you have a life-altering event where your life was derailed, and you have an inability or lack of desire to begin picking things up from before the tragedy occurred.
- Conventional organization methods do not fit within your lifestyle.
- You need a strategy tailored to your specific lifestyle and personality to find success with organization.

Does this sound like you, or maybe someone you know? If you think you might have something like this, you should consider reaching out to talk to your dedicated health professional. Don't be embarrassed about it because they can point you in the right direction and confirm if your problem is medical in nature. You can fix both of these organizational issues through learning basic organizational skills and by removing physical and mental clutter from your life.

Sometimes people use the excuse of a medical issue to avoid issues entirely. *Don't* do this to yourself. If you have a medical issue, *you* have to manage it and take responsibility for it. Don't use it as an excuse; instead, own up to it and find ways to work with it or around it. If you need a specific strategy to organize, then do what works for you rather than saying, *Well, I have OCD, so regular organizing doesn't work for me. I might as well just give up.*

If you need help or assistance, see a therapist. Asking for help, especially when you need it, is a sign of strength. It shows that you are aware enough to know that you cannot do everything, and you've put your ego aside in order to benefit yourself and the people around you. Keeping yourself in a healthy state of body and mind may not always be easy, though. Work and family may often keep you eating quick meals or finding convenient ways to excuse yourself from exercise, or even putting off your annual check-up.

Finding Health Improvements

To have proper balance in your life, you will need to fuel your body with the right nutrition. Eating a balanced and whole diet, incorporating supplements, creating a regular exercise routine, getting annual check-ups, building good sleeping habits, and drinking enough water are all things you can start doing to take back control.

Controlling Diet

While these ideas sound easy, and you may have already tried to incorporate them into your daily habits, actually pulling it off can be a little more difficult at times. Learning how to build a healthier life is going to take some commitment and some research. To start you off, I've compiled a list of scientifically proven tips that will help you get into the right rhythm and to start building your health life pillar.

First, although you can stay hydrated in many ways, drinking water is the best way to do it. Water has no calories, no sugar, and no additives. Water is an absolute necessity in your body for hydrating your cells, regulating body temperature, and creating blood, among many other things. Contrary to popular belief, everyone needs different levels of hydration and instead of focusing on drinking a certain amount of water a day, just drink enough to quench your thirst.

To this end, limit your intake of sugary drinks. Studies have found that when you often incorporate sweetened teas or sodas into your lifestyle, you run the risk of developing type 2 diabetes and heart disease. This can happen no matter what you weigh. Instead, try unsweetened flavored teas, coffees, and sparkling water if you need a break from regular water.

The great news about coffee is that despite the constant back and forth conversation about it, it's actually full of health benefits for you. Coffee has an abundance of antioxidants and has been connected to a reduced risk of Alzheimer's disease, Parkinson's disease, and type 2 diabetes. The problem comes when you add extra sugar, flavored syrups, or high-calorie sweeteners to it. You can also drink an excessive amount of it, which will give you too much caffeine in your system and set you up for a crash later in the day, and too much caffeine can give you insomnia and heart palpitations. By sticking to four cups of coffee or less a day, you can avoid this.

Nutrition and Food Labels

Another step to take is to start reading nutrition labels to increase awareness of what you are putting into your body. If the ingredients are a paragraph long and there are words you do not understand or cannot pronounce, chances are these are additives that make the food or drink unhealthy.

As you read labels, steer clear of highly processed foods. Foods that are highly processed are significantly modified from their original state and full of artificial sweeteners, colors, flavors, refined sugars and oils, salt, and preservatives.

Highly processed foods are easy to overeat and will activate certain regions in your brain that relate to rewards. That's why fast-food, junk food snacks, and cakes taste so good, because they are designed to be addictive. Big companies *want* you to be addicted to these foods so you keep coming back for more and so that they have a steadier, more reliable consumer base that benefits their bottom line without benefitting *you* in the process.

Once you start eliminating highly processed foods, you're going to want to find some healthier meals. To get into a more nutritious meal plan, you'll need to get some healthy fatty foods into your diet. The best sources of good fats come from meat and fish. Try to incorporate one meal of meat or fish into your weekly dinner plans. By doing this, you'll be getting into a great habit of adding a healthy meal a week, which you can increase as you find more recipes you like. Healthy fats in salmon and tuna are abundant in acids like Omega-3. Fatty acids like Omega-3 will help reduce inflammation in illnesses like inflammatory bowel disease. This will also give you a good source of protein, which is a vital part of a healthy diet. Your body uses protein to create new cells and tissue. Animal protein works perfectly, but some other high protein food examples are eggs, oats, broccoli, quinoa, and nuts (especially almonds).

On that note, nuts also contain healthy fats, protein, and fiber, along with several other micronutrients to help your body work correctly. Nuts also help reduce the risk of heart disease and type 2 diabetes. Giving yourself a handful of seeds as a snack can also help prevent strokes.

By switching out one snack a day for nuts and seeds, you can start to build a healthier habit and step into the mindset that nuts and seeds are snacks. If you don't like nuts or seeds, you can get natural bars that incorporate these ingredients with minimal additives and just enough sugar or peanut butter to hide the taste. Take note of the ingredients list on the snack bars: some companies advertise them as health bars, but the label will tell you otherwise and show you all the added sugars, dyes, and other hidden additives.

Lastly, you're going to want to start incorporating more fruits and vegetables into your diet. Research has found that people who eat more fruit and vegetables live longer and have a lower risk of heart disease, type 2 diabetes, obesity, and other diseases. There are an abundance of different choices out there, and even if you aren't a veggie fan, there's bound to be a handful you will enjoy!

Sleep and Relaxation

Eating well is one thing, but sleeping well is quite another. Developing good sleep hygiene is important for every aspect of your life; when you don't get enough sleep, it will interrupt your appetite and hormones, raise insulin resistance, and affect mental and physical performance. Also, when you are deprived of sleep, your day-to-day choices will be affected, including what you choose to eat. But how do you get enough sleep, let alone improve the quality of your sleep?

Turning off bright lights before you go to bed at night is a great way to help yourself get ready for a good sleep. Bright lights contain blue light wavelengths. Exposure to these types of wavelengths before you go to sleep has been found to disrupt melatonin production, which is a hormone needed to sleep. Avoiding bright lights about thirty minutes before you go to bed can help you relieve this issue.

Take control of your sleeping environment with blackout curtains to block out light in a temperature-controlled room. The bedding you sleep on also plays a major part in your sleep quality. Switching out a mattress, old pillows, or sheets for new or better quality ones could be the answer. Keep in mind that your bedroom should be the only place you associate with sleep. Specifically, your bed should only be used for two purposes: one of those is sleep!

Incorporating relaxing activities in the evening should also be considered in lieu of something that might make you angry, irritable, or stressed. The goal is to help clear your mind and reduce muscle tension to help you fall asleep faster and stay asleep. Maybe one of these natural remedies could be your simple solution?

- Reading a good book
- Aromatherapy
- A warm bubble bath
- Playing relaxing music or sounds of nature
- Guided imagery, meditation, or yoga
- Deep breathing exercises
- Writing or journaling
- Herbal teas such as camomile tea
- Natural supplements such as melatonin or valerian root

Exercise

You might hear this word and start panicking because the thought of doing physical exercise is totally beyond you. Let me remind you: it's not! Exercise requires about as much commitment as healthy eating, and it's a habit to get into, just like anything else we've covered. Exercise is not just about working out. Even doing light stretching before you sleep can help you relax your muscles and help you improve your sleep. Doing yoga in the morning can improve your mood, taking an afternoon walk in the park can be relaxing, and going for a light jog on a spring evening can leave you feeling much better afterward.

Different exercises have different purposes. Going for a run, for example, improves your cardiac health. Swimming can help to train your endurance and regulate your breathing. Stretching loosens your muscles after they've been tense or in a single position for a while. Both books and the internet are a great way to find different kinds of exercises that fit what you want to do, as well as whatever you feel comfortable doing.

Some people don't like the idea of exercise because they feel judged by others for their body or their efforts. Know that you don't have to feel judged! You can do just about any exercise in the comfort of your home so long as you have a big enough space. Pushups, situps, stretches, and the like can all be done without having to purchase a gym membership or be out in public at all, and you certainly don't need a home gym for them either! If you have an apartment, you may need to clear a space to do exercises, and you can even work that into your exercise routine. For example, if you have to move the couch out of the middle of your apartment for your exercise, make time to do a few minutes of stretching, move the couch, do your exercises, then do a few more minutes of stretching before you push the couch back!

If you've been sedentary for a while or haven't really been doing exercise, I recommend you start slow. Don't just jump into going for an hour-long run every day, or else you'll end up sore and tired. You're less likely to want to keep going if you wake up and everything hurts. With something like running as an example, if your goal is to go for a thirty-minute run each day, you'll want to walk ten minutes a day for the first week to get your body used to movement, then transition into fifteen minutes of walking for the second week, then do twenty minutes of walking for the third week. By week four you'll be doing five minutes of running and fifteen minutes of walking, in week five you'll do ten minutes of running and ten minutes of walking, and so on, until you can do a thirty-minute run each day. Make the transition slowly and don't be frustrated by your pace. You'll look back and see just how far you've come, and if you're not pleased with where you are and you want to keep pushing your limits, you just proved that you can do it!

Your "Health" Steps

Assess Your Situation

Let's break down the four main points of health: diet, exercise, sleep, and relaxation. Ask yourself where you are and what your weaknesses are in these four categories.

All but the healthiest people lament that they don't eat as well as they should or don't exercise as often as they should. Think about your current diet. Is it mostly burgers and fries or other quick, easy meals? What about your snacking habits? What do you reach for when you need a little pick-me-up? The same thing goes for exercise. Ask yourself where you are now. Are you mostly sedentary and getting out of your chair to get a drink is enough to annoy you? Do you do easy exercises like walking and stretching? Are you doing any strenuous exercises?

How much sleep on average are you getting a night? Be honest with yourself, is it a restful sleep or are you waking up multiple times in the night? Why? Is it a need to use the bathroom, nightmares, or loud noises inside or outside your house? Take a moment to think about your nighttime routine. Do you stress because you worry about having a hectic morning and find that it keeps you awake, or is there something else that keeps you from relaxing?

Evaluate What You Want

Think about where you want to improve. Write down any goals you would like to accomplish in your journal. You have to map out concrete goals for yourself for this pillar. Here, having set figures can help you more than in your other pillars, such as setting a goal to lose twenty pounds or doing thirty minutes of exercise each day. If you want to go on a diet, what are you hoping to achieve? Using scales and measuring tape, document your weight and height. Start by researching what your BMI (Body Mass Index) is. This will give you a good starting point to determine if you are in a healthy weight category or need to get there. Are you looking to lose weight? If so, set a goal for how much weight you want to lose. If you have any known health conditions, such as diabetes, anxiety, or heart conditions, you should make note of them as a focus point. Consider also getting some tests scheduled with your doctor if you suspect you may be developing an underlying health condition.

When it comes to exercise, ask yourself how much exercise you are getting weekly. Are you involved in any clubs or outdoor activities? Remember cleaning, gardening, home maintenance, and walking the dog all count as exercise. If you lead a largely sedentary lifestyle, consider setting aside a bit of time to do some stretching, or at least use that age-old tip of getting up and out of your chair once every twenty minutes. This is easier for some than others depending on your energy levels and your office setup; if you have a personal printer and a coffee machine right at your desk, you have pretty much no reason to get up. On the other hand, if the break room is about fifty yards away from your desk and the copier is about twenty yards away from your desk, of course you have more reasons to get up. Don't be grouchy if the latter is your setup—it can work to your advantage!

Once you evaluate what you are searching for, you will have to research how to get to what you want. If you want to go vegetarian, for example, you'll need to look for meatless recipes you can use. There are innumerable websites and nutrition books that can give you more in-depth information on what you want in greater detail, so you may need to use different sources for your information. Once you do this, the next step will be to put your research into motion.

Plan How to Get Results

For getting started on a healthier you, you'll need a plan. Get started by writing out a meal plan for the week. Consider utilizing meals that are versatile and can stretch for the week as designated leftover days on your calendar. Some examples are stews, Crock-Pot meals, casseroles, and lasagna-style dishes. If we look at lasagna, we can tailor this dish to our desired diet by changing up some simple ingredients. Imagine the possibilities: a no-noodle vegetable lasagna, a gluten-free lasagna, or a keto-friendly lasagna! If you have recipes that you want to try, first check and see if you have the ingredients. If not, start a shopping list for them, and whatever you do, *never* go food shopping when you are hungry! More than likely you will end up buying things you don't need, or you won't stick to your new plan.

When it comes to reducing junk food in your life, start cutting out small things you can part with. For example, plan to reduce your coffee additives each week. If you have two spoonfuls of sugar in a coffee, only have one and a half for the first week, and then cut it down again to one spoonful for the next week. This will help your body adjust and you'll be more likely to stick with it.

Plan out a routine on your calendar to follow for your exercise, even if it is as simple as "walk the dog three times a week." In your research, you may have found cardio exercises that will help you build up to that half-marathon you want to run, or specific exercises that will help with muscle toning. Start small and work your way up to more intensive exercise. Plan what exercise you want to do, how long you want to do it each day, when you want to do it in the day, and if you want to switch to a different exercise weekly or work up to more intensive exercise of the same type. Don't buy a gym membership just yet; do your exercises at home for now. If you can work a daily gym visit into your routine and you want to find like-minded people who enjoy exercise, it might be worthwhile for you.

After your busy day, make a plan of how you are going to wind down in the evenings. Are you intending to take a relaxing bath after your exercise? Does a steaming cup of chamomile tea and a good book sound better? Plan out the times each day you want to implement your chosen relaxing activity on the calendar and stick to the schedule. As for sleeping, plan out how you are going to accomplish that desirable night's sleep, whether that's through a fresh set of sheets, using natural sleeping aids, or a bit of meditation and self-reflection before settling down.

Take Action

Keep a weekly documentation on how your goals are coming along. For example, if you are trying to lose weight, step on the scale at the end of every week, and note that number in your calendar. If you are trying to build endurance, note down the increased time you could walk, jog, or hike for.

We get hit with so many advertisements for different junk food each day: fast-food, coffee, sports drinks, cereals, and candy. It's hard to not want to cave and just run out to buy a burger for lunch, but here's where honesty and accountability come in again. You have to hold yourself accountable for what you eat. If you eat this junk food weekly, or even daily, it won't be an easy habit to kick. If you see these advertisements on TV or hear them on the radio, change the channel. Tune them out if you see or hear them when you're driving. If you have sugary snacks in your house, have someone eat them or hide them so you're not looking at them every day. Some people stress-eat when they're overwhelmed or upset. Anytime you're tempted with an unhealthy food, ask yourself, *Is that really the healthiest thing I could eat right now?* If the answer is no, put it somewhere you can't see it and pick up something else.

The exercises won't be easy at first. Make a point of doing them before you go to work, on your break, after work, or before you go to bed. Take a morning constitutional, walk your dog after dinner, go for a jog in the park around noon, or do sit ups just before bed. Whatever exercise you've planned out will work best if you stick to it at a set time every day. You can tell yourself you'll stop exercising at the end of the week, but you might just find yourself saying, *One more day, I'll stop tomorrow*, which turns into another day, and another, until you've built it into your routine.

There will be times when you won't feel like following through on your goals such as exercising or eating healthy. When this happens, take a moment to think about if something is bothering you. More often than not, there will be an underlying issue. Ask yourself if the issue is worth breaking the progress you've accomplished. Change up your routine as you planned previously. Make your meal plans, buy your ingredients, switch out your exercises, and have your family or friends keep tabs on how you're doing. Keep going past the twenty-one-day mark, and you'll have started building healthy habits.

Reassess Your Progress

It may take a long time to build up stamina and develop a taste for healthier habits, but chances are when you go to reassess your progress, you'll be surprised at how far you've come. When you reassess your progress, consider the following:

1. What have you done so far?
2. How are you feeling? Where do you think you did well? What might need improvement?
3. What is the biggest healthy habit you've tackled? How did you do it? Is it a method that you can use when you're working on building your next habits?
4. What is your next goal?

This pillar check-in is crucial for success. Keeping that momentum is the key. A quick cheat day can leave you feeling guilty and you might not find the momentum to keep going. You will find yourself saying, *I'll start back up tomorrow*, but you never will. If it turns out that you took a step back from your healthy lifestyle, own up to it, regain control quickly, and get back on track. Trying new foods, pushing your limits with exercise, and implementing new relaxation techniques will all be part of the path to success. There will be some things you don't like so much and other things you love, and that's okay. When working on your health pillar, as the saying goes, "slow and steady wins the race."

FINAL WORDS

Dear Reader:

I wanted to thank you for taking this journey with me. You found out, as I did, that clutter is more than just a heap of dirty dishes or a pile of messy sheets. Clutter is both mental and physical in nature and it can cause your life to crash around you if you're not careful, but you took the time to look at the problems and take steps to correct them. This inner reflection is the drive to succeed. When you can find the source of the problem and proactively implement a solution, you are able to reach your fullest potential.

You built a strong foundation, improved upon it, and in doing so, you earned your own happiness. Throughout your journey, you will have experienced both success and failure. You may not have succeeded the first time; there were mistakes, setbacks, and lessons learned, as there will be going forward. Failure is only a setback— it's not a definite end until you give up. Taking what you learned and implementing it in the best way to help you grow and achieve your potential has made you a wiser, stronger person, and remember that you can always improve from where you are.

This journey was not easy. Going forward, it will require continuous application of the knowledge you've acquired. Remember that you are a better person for it. You are healthier, stronger, and more content for having taken steps toward improving yourself.

I wholeheartedly encourage you to tweak these methods to better fit your life. Reflect on the new things you've learned. Prioritize the things that matter most to you to help you lead the most fulfilling life you can.

Here and now, *you* are in control of your life, and only you can make the most of it. Now more than ever, you are ready to make your mark on the world. Make your voice heard, achieve your own greatness, and most importantly, find your freedom.

To your success,

Leah Novak

RESOURCES

Anxiety and Depression Association of America. 2000. "Physical Activity Reduces Stress | Anxiety and Depression Association of America, ADAA." Adaa.org. 2000. https://adaa.org/understanding-anxiety/related-illnesses/other-related-conditions/stress/physical-activity-reduces-st.

Bealing, Jacqui. 2014. "Brain Scans Reveal 'Gray Matter' Differences in Media Multitaskers." EurekAlert! September 24, 2014. https://www.eurekalert.org/news-releases/467495.

Bechthold, Angela, Heiner Boeing, Carolina Schwedhelm, Georg Hoffmann, Sven Knüppel, Khalid Iqbal, Stefaan De Henauw, et al. 2017. "Food Groups and Risk of Coronary Heart Disease, Stroke and Heart Failure: A Systematic Review and Dose-Response Meta-Analysis of Prospective Studies." *Critical Reviews in Food Science and Nutrition* 59 (7): 1071–90. https://doi.org/10.1080/10408398.2017.1392288.

Becker. 2019. "10 Creative Ways to Declutter Your Home." Www.becomingminimalist.com. October 22, 2019. https://www.becomingminimalist.com/creative-ways-to-declutter/.

"Bedroom Poll." *National Sleep Foundation*. 2012. https://www. sleepfoundation.org/wp-content/uploads/2018/10/2012-bedroom-poll.pdf?x11801.Bailey, Regan, Victor Fulgoni, Alexandra Cowan, and P. Gaine. 2018. "Sources of Added Sugars in Young Children, Adolescents, and Adults with Low and High Intakes of Added Sugars." *Nutrients* 10 (1): 102. https://doi.org/10. 3390/nu10010102.

Bradberry, Travis. n.d. "Multitasking Damages Your Brain and Your Career, New Studies Suggest." TalentSmart. https://www. talentsmarteq.com/articles/Multitasking-Damages-Your-Brain-and-Your-Career.

Carter, Sherrie Bourg Psy.D. "Why Mess Causes Stress: 8 Reasons, 8 Remedies." 2012. Psychology Today. 2012. https://www. psychologytoday.com/us/blog/high-octane-women/201203/why-mess-causes-stress-8-reasons-8-remedies.

Chan. 2017. "The Importance of Hydration." News. September 28, 2017. https://www.hsph.harvard.edu/news/hsph-in-the-news/the-importance-of-hydration/.

Cherry, Kendra. 2009. "The Health Consequences of Loneliness." Verywell Mind. 2009. https://www.verywellmind.com/loneliness-causes-effects-and-treatments-2795749.

Cherry, Kendra. 2020. "Social Support Is Imperative for Health and Well-Being." Verywell Mind. April 14, 2020. https://www. verywellmind.com/social-support-for-psychological-health-4119970.

Chisholm, Rupert F. 1983. "Quality of Working Life: Critical Issue for the 80s." *Public Productivity Review* 7 (1): 10. https://doi.org/10. 2307/3380357.

Cohut, Ph.D., Maria. 2018. "Socialization: How Does It Benefit Mental and Physical Health?" Www.medicalnewstoday.com.

February 23, 2018. https://www.medicalnewstoday.com/articles/321019?c=24611997694.

COING Inc. n.d. "Work/Life Quality and Work/Life Balance Guide." Clockify. https://clockify.me/work-life-quality-balance.

Constantine Tsigos, Ioannis Kyrou, Eva Kassi, and George P Chrousos. 2016. "Stress, Endocrine Physiology and Pathophysiology." Nih.gov. MDText.com, Inc. March 10, 2016. https://www.ncbi.nlm.nih.gov/books/NBK278995/.

Coulson, J.C. J. McKenna, M. Field. "Exercising at work and self–reported work performance" 2008. *Emerald Insight*.

"CUergo: Sitting and Standing." n.d. Ergo.human.cornell.edu. http://ergo.human.cornell.edu/CUESitStand.html.

Cutting, James E., and Kacie L. Armstrong. 2016. "Facial Expression, Size, and Clutter: Inferences from Movie Structure to Emotion Judgments and Back." *Attention, Perception, & Psychophysics* 78 (3): 891–901. https://doi.org/10.3758/s13414-015-1003-5.

Davis, Jeanie Lerche. n.d. "America, It's Time for Your Nap." WebMD. https://www.webmd.com/sleep-disorders/features/america-its-time-for-your-nap.

"DSM-V: Hoarding New Mental-Disorder Diagnoses." 2013. Promises Behavioral Health. May 3, 2013. https://www.promisesbehavioralhealth.com/addiction-recovery-blog/dsm-v-hoarding-new-mental-disorder-diagnoses/.

De Grip, Andries, and Jan Feld. 2013. "Research Report Optimism and Performance in Call Centers." http://www.networksocialinnovation.nl/nsi/wp-content/uploads/2013/02/Report-Optimism-and-Performance-in-Call-Centers.pdf.

Dickler, Jessica. 2021. "Americans Say They Need to Have $500,000 in Savings to Feel Financially Secure, Survey Finds." CNBC. July 28,

2021. https://www.cnbc.com/2021/07/28/americans-need-500000-in-savings-to-feel-financially-secure-survey-says.html.

Freedman, Neal D., Yikyung Park, Christian C. Abnet, Albert R. Hollenbeck, and Rashmi Sinha. 2012. "Association of Coffee Drinking with Total and Cause-Specific Mortality." *New England Journal of Medicine* 366 (20): 1891–1904. https://doi.org/10.1056/nejmoa1112010.

"FoodData Central." n.d. Fdc.nal.usda.gov. Accessed October 18, 2021. https://fdc.nal.usda.gov/fdc-app.html#/food-details/175167/nutrients.

Gibney, Michael J, Ciarán G Forde, Deirdre Mullally, and Eileen R Gibney. 2017. "Ultra-Processed Foods in Human Health: A Critical Appraisal." *The American Journal of Clinical Nutrition*, August, ajcn160440. https://doi.org/10.3945/ajcn.117.160440.

Gordon, Sherry. 2021. "Mental Health Benefits of Cleaning and Decluttering." Verywell Mind. February 23, 2021. https://www.verywellmind.com/how-mental-health-and-cleaning-are-connected-5097496#citation-1.

Gunnars, Kris. 2018. "13 Health Benefits of Coffee, Based on Science." Healthline. September 20, 2018. https://www.healthline.com/nutrition/top-13-evidence-based-health-benefits-of-coffee.

Hanley, Adam W., Alia R. Warner, Vincent M. Dehili, Angela I. Canto, and Eric L. Garland. 2014. "Washing Dishes to Wash the Dishes: Brief Instruction in an Informal Mindfulness Practice." *Mindfulness* 6 (5): 1095–1103. https://doi.org/10.1007/s12671-014-0360-9.

"The Health Benefits of Strong Relationships." 2010. Harvard Health. November 22, 2010. https://www.health.harvard.edu/staying-healthy/the-health-benefits-of-strong-relationships.

Haynes, Trevor. 2018. "Dopamine, Smartphones & You: A Battle for Your Time." Science in the News. May 1, 2018. https://sitn.hms. harvard.edu/flash/2018/dopamine-smartphones-battle-time/.

"Here Are Some Tips on How to Increase Workplace Productivity." https://www.facebook.com/thebalancecom. 2015. The Balance Small Business. 2015. https://www.thebalancesmb.com/top-ways-to-increase-productivity-2948669.

Hill, E. M., F. E. Griffiths, and T. House. 2015. "Spreading of Healthy Mood in Adolescent Social Networks." *Proceedings of the Royal Society B: Biological Sciences* 282 (1813): 20151180. https://doi.org/10.1098/rspb.2015.1180.

Hogan, Candice L., Jutta Mata, and Laura L. Carstensen. 2013. "Exercise Holds Immediate Benefits for Affect and Cognition in Younger and Older Adults." *Psychology and Aging* 28 (2): 587–94. https://doi.org/10.1037/a0032634.

Holt-Lunstad, Julianne, Timothy B. Smith, Mark Baker, Tyler Harris, and David Stephenson. 2015. "Loneliness and Social Isolation as Risk Factors for Mortality." *Perspectives on Psychological Science* 10 (2): 227–37. https://doi.org/10.1177/1745691614568352.

Holt-Lunstad, Julianne, Timothy B. Smith, and J. Bradley Layton. 2010. "Social Relationships and Mortality Risk: A Meta-Analytic Review." Edited by Carol Brayne. *PLoS Medicine* 7 (7): e1000316. https://doi.org/10.1371/journal.pmed.1000316.

"How to Manage Your Money: 6 Steps to Take." 2021. Www.us-bank.com. April 23, 2021. https://www.usbank.com/financialiq/plan-your-future/manage-wealth/balance-money.html.

"How Do You Stop Micromanaging?" https://www.facebook.com/thebalancecom. 2012. The Balance Small Business. 2012. https://www.thebalancesmb.com/how-to-stop-micromanaging-right-now-2951537.

Innovations, Mindwise. 2017. "How to Have a Healthy Relationship with Social Media." MindWise. July 31, 2017. https://www.mindwise.org/blog/mental-health/how-to-have-a-healthy-relationship-with-social-media/.

Kim, Jung Eun, Lauren E. O'Connor, Laura P. Sands, Mary B. Slebodnik, and Wayne W. Campbell. 2016. "Effects of Dietary Protein Intake on Body Composition Changes after Weight Loss in Older Adults: A Systematic Review and Meta-Analysis." *Nutrition Reviews* 74 (3): 210–24. https://doi.org/10.1093/nutrit/nuv065.

Kline, Christopher E, Martica H Hall, Daniel J Buysse, Conrad P Earnest, and Timothy S Church. 2018. "Poor Sleep Quality Is Associated with Insulin Resistance in Postmenopausal Women with and without Metabolic Syndrome." *Metabolic Syndrome and Related Disorders* 16 (4): 183–89. https://doi.org/10.1089/met.2018.0013.

Lane, Melissa M., Jessica A. Davis, Sally Beattie, Clara Gómez-Donoso, Amy Loughman, Adrienne O'Neil, Felice Jacka, et al. 2020. "Ultraprocessed Food and Chronic Noncommunicable Diseases: A Systematic Review and Meta–Analysis of 43 Observational Studies." *Obesity Reviews* 22 (3). https://doi.org/10.1111/obr.13146.

Liu, Qing-Ping, Yan-Feng Wu, Hong-Yu Cheng, Tao Xia, Hong Ding, Hui Wang, Ze-Mu Wang, and Yun Xu. 2016. "Habitual Coffee Consumption and Risk of Cognitive Decline/Dementia: A Systematic Review and Meta-Analysis of Prospective Cohort Studies." *Nutrition* 32 (6): 628–36. https://doi.org/10.1016/j.nut.2015.11.015.

Lang, Martin, Jan Krátký, John H. Shaver, Danijela Jerotijević, and Dimitris Xygalatas. 2015. "Effects of Anxiety on Spontaneous Ritualized Behavior." *Current Biology* 25 (14): 1892–97. https://doi.org/10.1016/j.cub.2015.05.049.

Marengo, Katherine LDN, R.D. "Valerian Root vs. Melatonin: Differences, and How Do They Help?" 2020. Www.medicalnewstoday.-

com. October 23, 2020. https://www.medicalnewstoday.com/articles/valerian-root-vs-melatonin.

McKeith, Nicole. 2012. "Tidier Homes, Fitter Bodies?: IU News Room: Indiana University." Iu.edu. 2012. https://newsinfo.iu.edu/web/page/normal/14627.html.

McMains, Stephanie, and Sabine Kastner. 2011. "Interactions of Top-down and Bottom-up Mechanisms in the Human Visual Cortex." *The Journal of Neuroscience* 31 (2): 587–97. https://doi.org/10.1523/JNEUROSCI.3766-10.2011.

Micha, Renata, Jose L. Peñalvo, Frederick Cudhea, Fumiaki Imamura, Colin D. Rehm, and Dariush Mozaffarian. 2017. "Association between Dietary Factors and Mortality from Heart Disease, Stroke, and Type 2 Diabetes in the United States." *JAMA* 317 (9): 912. https://doi.org/10.1001/jama.2017.0947.

Morgan, T. J. H., N. T. Uomini, L. E. Rendell, L. Chouinard-Thuly, S. E. Street, H. M. Lewis, C. P. Cross, et al. 2015. "Experimental Evidence for the Co-Evolution of Hominin Tool-Making Teaching and Language." *Nature Communications* 6 (1). https://doi.org/10.1038/ncomms7029.

Nair, Parvathy, and T Subash. 2019. "Quality of Work Life and Job Satisfaction: A Comparative Study." *International Journal of Business and Management Invention (IJBMI) ISSN.* https://www.ijbmi.org/papers/Vol(8)2/Series.%20I/C0802011521.pdf.

N. Gearhardt, Ashley, Caroline Davis, Rachel Kuschner, and Kelly D. Brownell. 2011. "The Addiction Potential of Hyperpalatable Foods." *Current Drug Abuse Reviewse* 4 (3): 140–45. https://doi.org/10.2174/1874473711104030140.

Ogilvie, Rachel P., and Sanjay R. Patel. 2017. "The Epidemiology of Sleep and Obesity." *Sleep Health* 3 (5): 383–88. https://doi.org/10.1016/j.sleh.2017.07.013.

P, Kotresh. 2020. "Quality of Work Life: Definition, Objectives, Factors, Models, Elements, Steps." Economics Discussion. May 19, 2020. https://www.economicsdiscussion.net/human-resource-management/quality-of-work-life/quality-of-work-life/32426.

Payne, Kevin. 2020. "Financial Documents: What to Save and What You Can Throw Away." Forbes Advisor. July 15, 2020. https://www.forbes.com/advisor/personal-finance/financial-documents-what-to-save-what-to-throw-away/.

Piedmont Healthcare "Is Clutter and Disorganization Hurting Your Health?" n.d. Www.piedmont.org. https://www.piedmont.org/living-better/is-clutter-and-disorganization-hurting-your-health.

Pereira, Dina. João Carlos Correia Leitão. Ângela Gonçalves. "Quality of Work Life and Organizational Performance: Workers' Feelings of Contributing, or Not, to the Organization's Productivity." 2019. *International Journal of Environmental Research and Public Health* 16(20). DOI:10.3390/ijerph16203803. (PDF) Quality of Work Life and Organizational Performance: Workers' Feelings of Contributing, or Not, to the Organization's Productivity (researchgate.net).

Rd, Mendonça, Pimenta Am, Gea A, de la Fuente-Arrillaga C, Martinez-Gonzalez Ma, Lopes Ac, and Bes-Rastrollo M. 2016. "Ultraprocessed Food Consumption and Risk of Overweight and Obesity: The University of Navarra Follow-up (SUN) Cohort Study." The American Journal of Clinical Nutrition. November 1, 2016. https://pubmed.ncbi.nlm.nih.gov/27733404/.

Robinson, Lawrence, and Melinda Smith. 2020. "Social Media and Mental Health." Https://Www.helpguide.org. HelpGuide. January 16, 2020. https://www.helpguide.org/articles/mental-health/social-media-and-mental-health.htm.

Ruairi Robertson, PhD. "The Top 9 Nuts to Eat for Better Health." 2018. Healthline. 2018. https://www.healthline.com/nutrition/9-healthy-nuts.

Saxbe, D. E., and R. Repetti. 2009. "No Place like Home: Home Tours Correlate with Daily Patterns of Mood and Cortisol." *Personality and Social Psychology Bulletin* 36 (1): 71–81. https://doi.org/10.1177/0146167209352864.

Seppälä, Emma. 2014. "The Power & Science of Social Connection: Emma Seppälä TEDx." Www.youtube.com. January 4, 2014. https://www.youtube.com/watch?v=WZvUppaDfNs.

S, Libby, and er. 2019. "This Is What It Means If a Messy Room Stresses You Out." Men's Health. January 23, 2019. https://www.menshealth.com/health/a26012549/clutter-messiness-stress-anxiety-health-psychology/.

Shultz, Susanne, Christopher Opie, and Quentin D. Atkinson. 2011. "Stepwise Evolution of Stable Sociality in Primates." *Nature* 479 (7372): 219–22. https://doi.org/10.1038/nature10601.

Soboleski, Sarah. 2020. "Compulsive Hoarding versus Chronic Disorganization." ClassicallyOrganized. March 13, 2020. https://www.classicallyorganized.com/post/compulsive-hoarding-versus-chronic-disorganization.

The Myers & Briggs Foundation. 2019. "The Myers & Briggs Foundation - Extraversion or Introversion." Myersbriggs.org. 2019. https://www.myersbriggs.org/my-mbti-personality-type/mbti-basics/extraversion-or-introversion.htm.

"The Top 9 Nuts to Eat for Better Health." 2018. Healthline. 2018. https://www.healthline.com/nutrition/9-healthy-nuts.

Torpy, Janet M., Cassio Lynm, and Richard M. Glass. 2007. "Chronic Stress and the Heart." *JAMA* 298 (14): 1722. https://doi.org/10.1001/jama.298.14.1722.

Vohs, Kathleen D., Joseph P. Redden, and Ryan Rahinel. 2013. "Physical Order Produces Healthy Choices, Generosity, and Conventionality, Whereas Disorder Produces Creativity." *Psychological Science* 24 (9): 1860–67. https://doi.org/10.1177/0956797613480186.

Wahl, Siegfried, Moritz Engelhardt, Patrick Schaupp, Christian Lappe, and Iliya V. Ivanov. 2019. "The Inner Clock—Blue Light Sets the Human Rhythm." *Journal of Biophotonics* 12 (12). https://doi.org/10.1002/jbio.201900102.

Wang, Tiange, Yoriko Heianza, Dianjianyi Sun, Yan Zheng, Tao Huang, Wenjie Ma, Eric B Rimm, et al. 2019. "Improving Fruit and Vegetable Intake Attenuates the Genetic Association with Long-Term Weight Gain." *The American Journal of Clinical Nutrition* 110 (3): 759–68. https://doi.org/10.1093/ajcn/nqz136.

"Work Life Balance | Mental Health America." 2019. Mhanational.org. 2019. https://www.mhanational.org/work-life-balance.

www.ingramcontent.com/pod-product-compliance
Lightning Source LLC
LaVergne TN
LVHW051417080426
835508LV00022B/3119